Reviews
The 5 Secrets to Social Success with Biblical Principles

"This morning I reviewed the fine manuscript of, *The 5 Secrets to Social Success with Biblical Principles.* Having previously sat in a couple of your classes and hearing you teach, I was anxious to see the full scope of your curriculum. Reading through the material, in the back of my mind I could hear you presenting the curriculum in your fun and engaging way!

It's obvious that a lot of time, prayer and study have gone into preparing *"The 5 Secrets to Social Success with Biblical Principles."* As I read through the manuscript, I could only think of how critical this material is to young people as they prepare for successful lives. I can see application of *"5 Secrets"* in schools, churches and for adults who are learning to transition out from social and economic poverty. The skills your curriculum teaches are the basic building blocks to healthy relationships which build social success in the home and beyond.

I am going to share your manuscript with Pastor Diane at our school, Leadership Christian Academy. Again, thank you for your dedication to Christ and to a cause which is so needed today. Blessings always,

James P. Dumont, Senior Pastor
Erie Christian Fellowship Church, Erie, Pennsylvania

In ministry there is a belief that we should not have conflict and that we should turn the other cheek and ignore. As you know this leads to no growth and stifles our opportunity to deal with and potentially resolve the conflict (communication) issues. I intend to use your materials immediately with our leadership team to set the stage for more Biblically based communication and conflict resolution. In honoring God we learn how to honor one another and each person's struggles and uniqueness.

Thanks for putting together these powerful training materials.
Blessings!

Dr. Jim Castleberry, Executive Director
The Cornerstone Rescue Mission, Rapid City, South Dakota

As the Program Director for a long-term transitional D & A program, I am always looking for classes that address the needs of those faced with constructing a recovery program that is concrete, practical and offers real life solutions to real life recovery issues.

We were blessed to have had Dr. Liken personally present this training to our clinical staff. Myself and staff found *The 5 Secrets to Social Success with Biblical Principles* a program to address the socialization and life skills issues that our men face grounded in Biblical principles.

This program addresses issues of isolation, thinking errors and attitude and explains Biblical directions for overcoming each issue. Each of these areas is a common pitfall for those trying to re-integrate back into society. We have already presented *The 5 Secrets to Success with Biblical Principles* program to our participants and the feedback was excellent. This program has legs!!

Darrell A. Smith B.S., C.A.C
Director of Programs and Men's Ministries
The Erie City Mission, Erie, Pennsylvania

"As a youth and young adult pastor, I spend a lot of time each week with the upcoming generation. I have found that a young person today is lacking fundamental people skills. They have lost the ability to talk with other people because technology and other mediums have removed the need for it. In one day, students now will text more words than they speak. They can also now avoid tough conversations and no longer have to look someone in the eye and shake a hand.

All they have to do is text, tweet, or Facebook the message. It is affecting how they relate to each other, their parents, and it is spilling over into the workforce. I have people tell me all the time that new hires today lack fundamental skills on resolving conflict and respecting the authorities placed over them.

The curriculum that Dr. Liken and Mrs. Blalock have written cuts right to the heart of this issue. It gives both practical and Biblical advice on how to overcome the social challenges that people face. This program can be used for many different age groups and will be effective at giving real world skills to those that need it desperately. Be blessed, this is truly well done."

Jason Ackerman, Student Ministry Pastor
Erie Christian Fellowship Church, Erie, Pennsylvania

"It is an honor being asked to write a testimonial to Lina's book *The 5 Secrets to Social Success with Biblical Principles.* I've known Lina for over 25 years in various roles, and in those 25+ years, she frequently talked of her desire to teach social skills to youth and those who never had the opportunity to learn healthy social skills. This work is a labor of love, and I believe, a fulfillment of that desire.

I have worked in the drug and alcohol field and private counseling, and it is evident that these skills are forgotten during the "lifestyle" and need to be relearned. This book is clearly written and can be utilized both in group format as well as individual. It can be an enormous tool for counselors of all disciplines in assisting teaching "right living". Applause to Lina for taking on this challenge and developing a winning formula."

Charen Pasky, LSW
ABC's of Building Better Lives, LLC Erie, Pennsylvania

"This is a great workbook for small groups and those volunteering and witnessing in our communities. *The 5 Secrets to Success with Biblical Principles Study Journal* reinforces God's Word in action with everyday life as it applies to each of us. Each step places us in real circumstances and provides applicable skills.

No matter where we are, or what we are doing, using Biblical principles and led by the Holy Spirit, we can genuinely and effectively communicate. Also, we cannot draw others to Christ, if we don't know how to relay the message.

Sheila Kern, Volunteer Coordinator and Single Parenting Ministries Facilitator
Fairview, Pennsylvania

"I will instruct you and teach you in the way you should
go: I will counsel you and watch over you."
Ps. 32:8

Establish

effective

social

skills

that

work

The 5 Secrets to SOCIAL SUCCESS

with **Biblical Principles**   Dr. Lina W. Liken, C.A.P *with* **Cali Blalock, B.S.**

WESTBOW
PRESS
A DIVISION OF THOMAS NELSON
& ZONDERVAN

Scriptures taken from the Holy Bible, New International Version®, NIV®. Copyright © 1973, 1978, 1984, 2011 by Biblica, Inc.™ Used by permission of Zondervan. All rights reserved worldwide. www.zondervan.com The "NIV" and "New International Version" are trademarks registered in the United States Patent and Trademark Office by Biblica, Inc.™ All rights reserved.

Scripture taken from the New King James Version. Copyright 1979, 1980, 1982 by Thomas Nelson, inc. Used by permission. All rights reserved.

Scripture quotations taken from the Holy Bible, New Living Translation, copyright 1996, 2004. Used by permission of Tyndale House Publishers, Inc., Wheaton, Illinois 60189. All rights reserved.

WestBow Press books may be ordered through booksellers or by contacting:

WestBow Press
A Division of Thomas Nelson & Zondervan
1663 Liberty Drive
Bloomington, IN 47403
www.westbowpress.com
1 (866) 928-1240

ISBN: 978-1-4908-2198-6 (sc)
ISBN: 978-1-4908-2199-3 (e)

Library of Congress Control Number: 2014901161

Printed in the United States of America.

WestBow Press rev. date: 2/3/2014

Contents

About the Authors

A gifted teacher in secular or Christian arenas, Lina Liken, Ed.D., CAP, is currently a full time Assistant Professor of General Education at South University Online. Dr. Liken holds a Master's and a Doctorate in Education and a Bachelor's in Psychology. She also is a Certified Addiction Professional in the state of Florida. Her background includes high school English and Social Studies Instructor and Guidance Counselor, a Psychology Instructor, and an Adult and Adolescent Rehabilitation Therapist. Her hobbies include serving in her church and community, editing for writers, watching her garden produce herbs and vegetables, and walking on the beach.

Dr. Liken created Liken & Associates, which encompasses her expertise in international consulting, curriculum design, delivery of addiction related topical modules, professional ethics, and group dynamics; also state regulations for treatment providers, organizational development, executive coaching, labor-management conflict resolution, and service on various union/management grievance committees.

Her curriculum design now centers on Biblically focused material that emphasizes strengthening the application of scriptural based life/social skills with Biblical principles as the foundation. Dr. Liken resides in Delray Beach, Florida/Erie, Pennsylvania.

Contact her at: DrL@likenandassociates.com

Cali Blalock, a multidimensional educator since 1996, instructs in various venues and capacities. Presently, she focuses her skills, talents and energies on the homeschool education of her four young children while serving as the Children's Ministry Director of Cornerstone Bible Fellowship in Delray Beach, Florida, under the leadership of Pastor Bernard King, Sr. By the power and leading of the Holy Spirit, her skills have enabled her to design, develop and deliver educationally effective curriculum.

As a homeschool educator, she is involved in her homeschool community serving as a tutor in a small group setting for elementary aged children through the Classical Conversations, a nationwide Christian homeschool community with a focus on knowing God and making Him known. On a weekly basis, she leads the exploration of multidisciplinary subjects, science, math, history and more with emphasis on the revelation of God through these concepts. Additionally, her service to homeschoolers includes professional evaluations of students at multiple levels; documenting and evaluating their yearly progress. Since June 2011 she serves at her church by supervising and engaging in the leading of instruction of God's children through exciting Bible lessons.

A 1996 graduate of Nyack College, Cali had a minor in Bible and earned a Bachelor of Science degree in Elementary Education. Cali and her husband, Christopher, and their five children reside in the Ft. Lauderdale, Florida area.

Contact her at: caliblalock@likenandassociates.com

Dear Program Participant:

Welcome to **The 5 Secrets to Social Success with Biblical Principles** program!

This Study Journal has been designed to simplify and strengthen your program experience. Using it will help to reinforce the essential skills being presented in **The 5 Secrets to Social Success with Biblical Principles** program.

Once you have completed the program and filled in your Study Journal, it also will provide a refresher for future reference.

Each part of the Study Journal contains information essential to being a participant in **The 5 Secrets to Social Success with Biblical Principles** program and then enjoying real-life social success.

Utilizing the steps in this Biblically based program will afford opportunities for identifying personal life/social strengths and areas for improvement in the core social skills, supportive of life success through life skills attainment. Once identification is completed, skill training can enhance existing strengths and transform areas for improvement into skill foundation, guided by Biblical principles.

This Study Journal includes:

- Instructions
- Study Guides
- Note-taking pages
- Assessment
- Reviews

When it is completed, the Study Journal will be your own personal study guide for **The 5 Secrets to Social Success with Biblical Principles** program skills.

Again, welcome. Enjoy, learn, and *succeed*!

In His service,
Dr. Lina W. Liken, C.A.P.
Cali Blalock, B.S.

Mission Statement

Our mission is to help Christian youth, adolescents, women, and men, develop into godly, effective, social beings, as sojourners in this world and citizens of heaven (*Philippians 3:20*).

We will accomplish this through teaching the guidelines and principles outlined in Scripture that provide training for valuable life and social skills, including powerful critical thinking skills, and strong, focused attitudes for success.

Our program stresses Biblical principles that equip believers to live respectful and productive lives, guided by compassion, righteousness, and integrity, utilizing the following skills targeted in ***THE 5 SECRETS TO SOCIAL SUCCESS WITH BIBLICAL PRINCIPLES.***

Communication
Civility
Humility
Relationships
Wisdom

Author/Director of Life Skills Education
Dr. Lina W. Liken
Educator
Certified Addictions Professional

Contributing Author /Biblical Consultant
Cali Blalock, B.S.
Educator

Editor
Kevin Hrebik, D.Min.

Nature of the Problem

S.I.N.
Severed fellowship with God in the Garden of Eden
Isolation encouraged and fostered through an ever developing technology
No understanding of individual purpose and function within a society

In the real world, as children and youth we either prepare for adult success, or we do not. When we do prepare, our achievements, planned for specific outcomes, are considered success.

As adults, who demonstrate evidence of ability to succeed in life, we embody certain characteristics, values, attitudes, competencies and skills.

The presenting problem is that many times as youth we have been side tracked during our usual preparatory years. As a result, our life success potential has been high-jacked. What is the force sidetracking us? There can be multiple obstacles sidetracking us during critical developmental years.

One of the results of being sidetracked and jeopardizing adequate life skills and social development is that as youth we arrive at adulthood unprepared or underprepared for social success. ***THE 5 SECRETS TO SOCIAL SUCCESS WITH BIBLICAL PRINCIPLES*** has been developed in response to this identified gap in life and social development, critical thinking skills and social awareness.

"I will instruct you and teach you in the way you should go;
I will counsel you and watch over you."
Psalm 32:8

Curriculum of Life Skills

Life/Socialization Skills
I. Communication

Core Competencies
1. Establishing Appropriate Eye Contact
2. Understanding Hearing, Listening, Attending
3. Conversing

II. Civility

Core Competencies
1. Using Humor in Conversation
2. Disagreeing Respectfully
3. Resolving Conflict
4. Remaining Calm

III. Humility

Core Competencies
1. Introducing Self and Others
2. Living with Manners
3. Showing Respect

IV. Relationships

Core Competencies
1. Reading Emotions
2. Persuading Others
3. Demonstrating Appropriate Affection during Conversation

Critical Thinking Skills
V. Wisdom

Core Competencies
1. Adopting and Demonstrating a Positive Attitude
2. Identifying Personal Values
3. Setting Attainable Goals
4. Making Effective Decisions
5. Developing a Personal Value-based Mission Statement

Establish

effective

social

skills

that

work

SECTION ONE

Life & Socialization Skills

with **Biblical Principles**

Liken & Associates

Introduction

What are They? Why are They Important?

DEFINITION: Those skills that support the ability to communicate, persuade, and interact with other members of the society, without undue conflict or disharmony.

We live in a society of other people which necessitates being able to live with them and among them, as essential to our survival, both personally and professionally. Therefore, it is in our best interest as individuals, and as members of social units, to have effective socialization skills to facilitate appropriate social interactions and communication. In social interactions, there are different roles.

We have identified three major types of socialization categories:
(1) Participant, (2) Observer, (3) Observer/Participant

In order to be successful in social situations, you must be a **participant**. When you are comfortable with the social processes, it is easier to move into the role of a **participant** where you are really a part of what is happening.

When could you be an **observer**? Sitting in a classroom, meeting, or lecture, without thinking about what is going on is an inappropriate **observer** role. Sitting at a soccer game, in the stands watching the game, would be an example of an appropriate time for being an **observer**.

When could you be an **observer/participant**? While at the above soccer game, you can be an **observer/participant** by cheering for your team. When you are a team member and it is not your turn to play, you can watch (**observe**) while thinking about the plays and anticipating what is coming next. The same principle applies in a classroom, meeting, or lecture.

ACTIVITY
1. **Discuss:** Social behavior. What is your understanding of what it is and why it could be important in your life at this point?
2. **Describe:** Social situations where you are a Participant, Observer, or Observer/ Participant.
3. Analyze: In any of those situations, would you prefer to have been more involved in what was going on around you?

Congratulations! You have begun the process of changing your life by thinking of how to be more socially comfortable.

Introduction to Biblical Principles

*Our Creator has implemented order and structure throughout
creation that requires us to utilize fundamental skills
to achieve harmony and success within society.*

Psalm 34:14 *Turn from evil and do good; seek peace and pursue it.*

Psalm 133:1 *How good and pleasant it is when brothers live together in unity!*

Jeremiah 29:7 *Also, seek the peace and prosperity of the city to which I have carried you into exile. Pray to the LORD for it, because if it prospers, you too will prosper.*

Romans 12:18 *If it is possible, as far as it depends on you, live at peace with everyone.*

Romans 14:19 *Let us therefore make every effort to do what leads to peace and to mutual edification.*

1 Corinthians 12:12-20 *Just as a body, though one, has many parts, but all its many parts form one body, so it is with Christ. For we were all baptized by one Spirit so as to form one body—whether Jews or Gentiles, slave or free—and we were all given the one Spirit to drink. Even so the body is not made up of one part but of many. Now if the foot should say, "Because I am not a hand, I do not belong to the body," it would not for that reason stop being part of the body. And if the ear should say, "Because I am not an eye, I do not belong to the body," it would not for that reason stop being part of the body. If the whole body were an eye, where would the sense of hearing be? If the whole body were an ear, where would the sense of smell be? But in fact God has placed the parts in the body, every one of them, just as he wanted them to be. If they were all one part, where would the body be? As it is, there are many parts, but one body.*

Hebrews 12:14 *Make every effort to live in peace with all men and to be holy; without holiness no one will see the Lord.*

BIBLE VERSIONS

Unless otherwise noted, all Scripture references in the Biblical Principles sections are taken from *The Holy Bible,* New International Version (NIV), ©1984 International Bible Society. Other versions used: New Living Translation (NLT), New King James Version (NKJV).

I

Communication

SKILL 1: Establishing Appropriate Eye Contact

DEFINITION: Looking directly at the person to whom you are listening, or to/with whom you are speaking.

Types of Eye Contact: **Friendly** and **Unfriendly**

Friendly eye contact encourages communication.

Friendly eye contact consists of looking straight at the other person(s), smiling and having a relaxed posture and open look on your face. When there is friendly eye contact, the other person(s) recognizes that you are interested in them and what they have to say.

It is important to establish eye contact in order to promote communication so that ideas can be exchanged. Not looking at a person who is speaking to you, or to whom you are speaking, is rude and sends a message of not regarding the person or what they are saying.

Unfriendly eye contact discourages communication and can end communication. At its worst, unfriendly eye contact can provoke anger and misunderstanding.

Unfriendly eye contact is when you stare, scowl, roll your eyes or sneer at someone. When those types of eye contact are used, the exchange of ideas cannot happen or cannot happen effectively.

ACTIVITY
1. **Role Play:** With a partner, begin a sentence to the other person, look them straight in the eye, and then look away as you continue to speak.
2. **Discuss:** Ask the other person how they felt when you looked away.
3. **Role Play:** Take turns using unfriendly eye contact, asking the other person how they feel after each example. Alternate with straightforward, direct, and friendly eye contact with each other.
4. **Analyze:** How did each of you feel this time?

Congratulations! You are moving forward to being
more effective in your social contacts.

<u>BIBLICAL PRINCIPLE</u>
*Believers should purpose to convey confidence, security,
honor, and respect to those with whom they interact.*

Psalm 119:18 *Open my eyes that I may see wonderful things in your law.*

Matthew 6:21-23 *The eye is the lamp of the body. If your eyes are healthy, your whole body will be full of light. But if your eyes are unhealthy, your whole body will be full of darkness. If then the light within you is darkness, how great is that darkness!*

Matthew 6:21-23 (NLT) *Your eye is a lamp for your body. A pure eye lets sunshine into your soul. But an evil eye shuts out the light and plunges you into darkness. If the light you think you have is really darkness, how deep that darkness will be!*

Romans 12:10 *Be devoted to one another in love. Honor one another above yourselves.*

<u>MEMORY VERSE</u>
1 Peter 2:17 *Show proper respect to everyone, love the family of believers, fear God, honor the emperor.*

STUDY GUIDE

DEFINITION: Looking directly at the person to whom you are listening, or to/with whom you are speaking.

Being willing to commit to appropriate eye contact opens the door for communication. Many times we are not willing to offer time and attention to another person with whom we have contact. Each opportunity for connecting with another opens the door for shining forth God's light.

1. Describe the goal of appropriate eye contact: [in your own words].

   _____

   _____

   _____

   _____

2. Describe how you have handled eye contact in the past and what circumstances determined it.

   _____

   _____

   _____

   _____

   _____

   _____

3. Think back to a time when you noticed poor or missing eye contact from someone you were in conversation with. What were your feelings?

   _____

   _____

   _____

   _____

<u>REVIEW</u>

Believers should purpose to convey confidence, security, honor, and respect to those with whom they interact.

1. *Fill in the Blanks:*
Matthew 6:21-23 describes the eye as the _____ of the _____.

2. *Circle the Correct Letter:*
According to Romans 12:10, how should we treat others?
    a. with great trepidation   b. with disrespect
    c. with hostility   d. with honor and devotion

According to 1 Peter 2:17, whom should we respect:
    a. our immediate family   b. those in authority
    c. God   d. all of the above

3. *Write :*
1 Peter 2:17 from memory on the lines below:

_____

_____

_____

_____

_____

_____

SKILL 2: Understanding Hearing, Listening, Attending

DEFINITIONS:

Hearing

Hearing is the first stage of listening. Hearing is strictly technical when your ear picks up sound waves transported to your brain. This is the sense of hearing; it is not planned – it just happens.

Listening

This is a choice that requires thinking and focusing, which leads to brain processing from the words and word combinations heard. Listening is part of a larger process and leads to learning. Active listening then leads to communication, which is an exchange of ideas, and when it is real it leads to attending.

Attending

This is listening while being actively involved in the process. This means that there is appropriate eye contact and ideas heard are clarified for understanding. The process includes openness and touches on feelings.

ACTIVITY
1. **Hearing:** One partner taps on a surface, either with their foot or hand, making a sound. You hear it. Have them whistle or make a coughing noise. You hear it. This is simple hearing.
2. **Listening:** Have your partner ask you a simple question: "What's your name and address?" They have put words together and your brain has processed meaning from not just hearing but listening to them. Now respond to the question, and then do the same for your partner. Listening is a vital part of communicating, which is a sharing of information and ideas.
3. **Attending:** Using proper eye contact from Skill 1, start with an open posture, facing your partner. Look directly at them and ask them a question about the weather. Whatever response they give, ask a clarifying question such as, "Are you happy with today's weather?" Beyond hearing and listening, you have begun the attending process. Trade roles now with your partner and repeat the entire process with them, following each step.
4. **Discuss:** When finished, discuss the three different stages of hearing, listening, and attending. Are you more aware now of the benefits of attending in the communication process? Is there a difference in this process from how you heard, listened, or attended before? Can you see any positive reason to use this skill in your communicating?

Congratulations! You are more prepared to listen and
attend when communicating with others.

BIBLICAL PRINCIPLE

Wisdom is an essential component of the Christian makeup. Attaining wisdom is accomplished through the disciplines of hearing, listening, and attending.

Exodus 15:26 *He said, "If you listen carefully to the LORD your God and do what is right in his eyes, if you pay attention to his commands and keep all his decrees, I will not bring on you any of the diseases I brought on the Egyptians, for I am the LORD, who heals you."*

Proverbs 4:1, 20 *Listen, my sons, to a father's instruction; pay attention and gain understanding. My son, pay attention to what I say; listen closely to my words.*

Proverbs 5:1-2 *My son, pay attention to my wisdom, listen to my words of insight, that you may maintain discretion and your lips may preserve knowledge.*

Proverbs 15:31 *He who listens to a life-giving rebuke will be at home among the wise.*

James 1:19 *My dear brothers, take note of this: everyone should be quick to listen, slow to speak and slow to become angry.*

MEMORY VERSE

Matthew 13:23 *But the seed falling on good soil refers to someone who hears the word and understands it. This is the one who produces a crop, yielding a hundred, sixty or thirty times what was sown.*

STUDY GUIDE

Answer the following questions about the song.

1. What instruments can you hear playing in the song?

   _____

   _____

   _____

2. Write some of the lyrics you listened to.

   _____

   _____

   _____

   _____

3. What was the message of the song? Discuss your results with a partner.

   _____

   _____

   _____

   _____

   _____

4. Review Matthew 13:18-23. Where do you see yourself in this passage of scripture? Is your heart the good soil that received the seed, understood it, and is now producing a good crop? Explain.

   _____

   _____

   _____

   _____

Have YOU received Christ as your Lord and Savior? _____

Do you need more understanding of what that means? _____

If so, ask to speak with one of your peers regarding salvation and the gospel message. This is your opportunity to receive more understanding.

REVIEW

Wisdom is an essential component of Christian character. Attaining wisdom is accomplished through learning the skills of hearing, listening, and attending.

1. *Circle the Correct Letter:*
According to Proverbs 4:1, what do we gain as a result of paying attention?
     a. headache   b. understanding   c. friendships   d. money

2. *List:*
The three pieces of advice found in James 1:19, which could be implemented when we are engaged in conversations with others.

    a. _____

    b. _____

    c. _____

3. *Write* :
Matthew 13:23 from memory on the lines below:

_____

_____

_____

_____

_____

_____

SKILL 3: Conversing

DEFINITION: Respectful exchange of ideas between two or more people . . . usually verbal, but in our world, sometimes written (texted or emailed).

When two or more people want to exchange ideas or hear what another person thinks or knows, a process begins where words are traded. In order for this process to be of use to each party, there must be guidelines for respect.

> **Discussion:** When you have a conversation, what is it that you want from the other person? What happens when your needs are not met in that encounter, such as the other party not understanding what you are talking about, not allowing you to finish your thoughts, or dismissing your conversation in some disrespectful way?

ACTIVITY
Scene 1. Pair up with a partner and discuss the weather. Have a third person join in and interrupt them, talking about the meal they just had, or perhaps a sports game, or something else completely unrelated.
Scene 2. Divide into groups of three or four and discuss a topic on which all can contribute.
Compare: Some report back to the group how the second scene went and felt as compared to the first scene.
Discuss: In the group describe how did these encounters feel? Did any real conversation take place?

Congratulations! You are moving forward into the world of successful socialization skills, building your awareness of effective conversation experiences.

BIBLICAL PRINCIPLE

*Christ engaged his audience with speech filled with purpose,
authority, wisdom, and compassion. His words instructed,
corrected, enlightened, edified, and encouraged his listeners.*

Psalm 19:14 *May the words of my mouth and the meditation of my heart be pleasing in your sight, O LORD, my Rock and my Redeemer.*

Psalm 34:12-13 *Whoever of you loves life and desires to see many good days, keep your tongue from evil and your lips from speaking lies.*

Proverbs 4:24 *Put away perversity from your mouth; keep corrupt talk far from your lips.*

Proverbs 8:6-8 *Listen, for I have worthy things to say; I open my lips to speak what is right. My mouth speaks what is true, for my lips detest wickedness. All the words of my mouth are just; none of them is crooked or perverse.*

Proverbs 15:7 *The lips of the wise disperse knowledge, But the heart of the fool does not do so.*

James 3:9-10 *With the tongue we praise our Lord and Father, and with it we curse human beings, who have been made in God's likeness. Out of the same mouth come praise and cursing. My brothers and sisters, this should not be.*

MEMORY VERSE

Ephesians 4:29 (NKJV) *Let no corrupt word proceed out of your mouth, but what is good for necessary edification, that it may impart grace to the hearers.*

Idle Talk Script

Players: 4 Friends, Radio DJ, friendly neighbor
Setting: Front porch on a lazy summer afternoon
Background: A few of John's close buddies happen to stop by and join him during a hot summer afternoon to pass the time.

(John walks out onto his front porch with a soda in hand, a small electric fan, and a small battery operated radio playing music from the local radio station, Slander 101.5. *He plugs in his fan, plops down on one of the rockers and takes a sip from his soda.)*

Radio DJ: (enthusiastically) Folks, have you heard the latest? Hollywood's latest ... headlines out of the *National Slanderer* confirm that Brady Pitz catches his beloved, Angela Josie, in yet another compromising predicament. Stay tuned after this set for the juicy details! Here's Goo-goo Baby with *Tell Me More!*

(Radio fades into background as John's friends Nick, Ray, and Scott arrive.)

Nick, Ray, Scott: John! S'up?

John: Just relaxin', catching some tunes and news on the box.

Ray: (sarcastically) Don't knock yourself out workin' too hard. We know how hard you like to work.

John: (cynically) What'cha'll up to?

Scott: Nut'in. Bored. It's hot! Not too much to do.

Nick: Too hot to even move.

John: Have some soda and chill. (John opens a small cooler sitting on the porch and hands his friends each a soda.)

(Friends all sit and sip at their sodas. Just then, John's neighbor passes by and enthusiastically greets John and his friends.)

Neighbor: Hey, Guys! How d'ya like this weather? Hot enough for ya'?

John: (sarcastically) Yeah, yeah. Real hot. How's it going, neighbor? How are the kids, and your wife Sally?

Neighbor: You mean, Sarah. She's great. Thanks. Just got home from the hospital last week. You know we're on baby #5. Our little man is doing great and Sarah is as beautiful as ever. We're so blessed. I'll let her know you asked about her.

John: Yeah, yeah, you do that. Where're *you* off to?

Neighbor: Need to run to the store. We're out of diapers and Sarah is craving some chocolate. Gotta keep my little lady happy, you know. She's a real treasure. You guys have a great day and try to stay cool. God bless.

John, Nick, Ray, Scott: (Lazily waving) Sure, sure. You too. Blessings and all that good stuff.

Scott: (Exclaiming) WHAT! Five kids!!!

Nick: (chiming in) Don't they have T.V.??

Ray: Apparently not!

Scott: (unsure) Well ... at least he seems like a nice enough guy.

Nick: He'd have to be with 5 kids AND a woman!

John: Don't let his charm fool you, fellas. I'm sure he's making an extra stop before he makes it home to momma and the kids. A man's gotta keep his sanity.

Ray: I betcha' right. I wouldn't be surprised if he has himself another little fling for convenience on the other side of town.

Nick: Come to think of it, I do recall seeing him at the grocery store while I was waiting in line, minding my own business, reading the *National Slanderer*, and noticing that he was a little too friendly with the cashier.

John: Which one?

Scott: It was probably the one who wears all that make-up and has all those tattoos.

Nick: (nodding his head slowly, seeming a little unsure) Could've been.

Ray: Naaahhh! She's too young!

John: (before he takes a sip) I wouldn't put it past him. Heard she's been around too.

Nick, **Ray**, **Scott**: (before taking sips of their own soda and nodding slowly) True, true.

(Radio becomes more audible)

Radio DJ: You guessed it folks! She's filing for divorce because she's tired of living a lie. Angela loves another! Now crank up your volume and tune in to Puffy Momma's latest release *Lies We Believe.*

Conversations of Love Script

Players: 4 Friends, Radio DJ, neighbor/Fred
Setting: Front lawn on a hot summer afternoon
Background: A few of John's close buddies stop by and join him during a hot summer afternoon to help him with weeding and landscaping.

(John walks out onto his front lawn with a water bottle, a small electric fan, and a small battery operated radio playing music from the local Christian radio station, God Speaks 191.4. *He plugs in his fan, takes a sip from his water, puts on his gloves and begins weeding).*

Radio DJ: (enthusiastically) Folks, have you heard? Proverbs 8:6-8 says, *Listen for I have worthy things to say; I open my lips to speak what is right. My mouth speaks what is true, for my lips detest wickedness. All the words of my mouth are just; none of them is crooked or perverse!* Here's Fifth Day with *The Words of My Heart!*

(Radio fades into background as John's friends Nick, Ray, and Scott arrive.)

Nick, Ray, Scott: John! S'up?

John: Just getting started. Listenin' to some uplifting tunes to get me going.

Ray: Well ... don't get started without us. We know you're a hard worker and God blesses you for the work of your hands ...

Scott: ... but we're here to "bear one another's burdens". There's too much to do for just one person.

John: Have some water and dig in. Thanks. (John opens a small cooler sitting on the porch and hands his friends each a water.)

(Friends all sip their waters and put on gloves to begin working. Just then, John's neighbor passes by and enthusiastically greets John and his friends.)

Neighbor: Hey, Guys! How d'ya like this weather? Hot enough for ya'?

John: (enthusiastically) Hey, Fred! Yes, it's very hot. How's it going? How are the kids, and your wife, Sarah?

Neighbor/Fred: Sarah's not doing too well. She just got home from the hospital last week. You know we're on baby #5. Our little man is doing great but Sarah is having a hard time because of the C-section.

John: I'm so sorry to hear that. I'll ask my wife to pass by later and check on her. Perhaps we can bring you all a meal and help a little around the house. Where're *you* off to?

Neighbor/Fred: Need to run to the store. We're out of diapers and Sarah needs some pain killers. I'm afraid I'm not much help. I have to go back to work this week cause we're falling behind on the bills. Don't know if I'll be able to pay the mortgage this month. Listen, don't want to burden you. You guys have a great day and try to stay cool. (Directing his attention to John's friends; Fred hurries off.)

John, Nick, Ray, Scott: (concerned) Sure, sure. God bless, man.

Scott: (Exclaiming) Praise God! Five kids!!! You know scripture teaches that children are a reward.

Nick: That's true. Don't know what I did to deserve my three but I'm grateful to have them.

Ray: It sounds like your neighbor needs some encouragement!

Scott: And some help! What can we do?

Nick: First, we pray. The book of James teaches, *"If any of you lacks wisdom, he should ask God, who gives generously to all without finding fault, and it will be given to him"*.

John: Don't let his appearance fool ya' fellas. I'm sure he's having a harder time than he's letting show. You know how it is. A man's gotta keep his faith in uncertain times.

Ray: I betcha' right. Maybe there's a "Honey-Do" list somewhere we could help out with.

Nick: Come to think of it, I do recall seeing his home halfway painted on the outside.

John: I know he has some paint in his garage. Let's go on over to his place and start working.

Scott: I'll also talk to my church to see if there's anyway to help out with his mortgage this month.

Nick: (nodding his head) Great idea.

Ray: Men! *"A generous man will prosper; he who refreshes others will himself be refreshed."* Proverbs11:25.

ALL: (Take sips of their water) True, true.

(Radio becomes more audible)

Radio DJ: *"Let no corrupt word proceed out of your mouth, but what is good for necessary edification, that it may impart grace to the hearers."* Ephesians 4:29. Are your words teaching, edifying and encouraging others? Here's Mick Tobias with *Gracious Words.*

STUDY GUIDE

DEFINITION: Respectful exchange of ideas... between two or more people... usually verbal, but in our world, sometimes written (texted or emailed).

Answer the following questions after thoughtful consideration of your idea:.

1. Choose one of your current relationships and consider how it could benefit from more effective conversations:

    _____

    _____

    _____

    _____

    _____

2. Remember one recent conversation that you were involved in when it didn't go the way you wanted it to. What could you have changed on your part that could have changed how the conversation ended:

    _____

    _____

    _____

    _____

    _____

REVIEW

Christ engaged his audience with speech filled with purpose, authority, wisdom, and compassion. His words instructed, corrected, enlightened, edified, and encouraged his listeners.

1. *Fill in the Blank:*

According to Psalm 19:14, the words we speak should first be pleasing to _____.

2. *True or False:*

_____Ephesians 4:29 teaches that our words should be used to express our opinions and for praising ourselves.

3. *Circle the Correct Letter:*

What is the promise of Psalm 34:12-13 if we keep our tongues from evil and our lips from speaking lies?

      a. we would enjoy many good days
      b. our financial status will improve
      c. many will come to seek our counsel
      d. all of the above

4. *Fill in the Blanks:*

According to James 3:9-10, _____ and _____ should not come out of the same mouth.

Proverbs 15:7 explains that a wise person disperses _____ with their words.

      a. sarcasm   b. insult   c. attitude   d. knowledge

II

Civility

SKILL 1: Using Appropriate Humor in Conversation

DEFINITION: Enjoying sharing humor with others, having fun, yet not upsetting or insulting anyone/anything, present or absent.

When humor is shared and jokes are told, the respectful goal should be that everyone can laugh and not feel embarrassed for themselves or others, present or not. What this means is that some topics, such as body parts, body functions, and nationality and other groups are not part of the humor. The list of "do not's" would include using obscene language or gestures. This practice is rude and can be hurtful, and it does not reflect the previous social skill of being respectful.

Note that sarcastic remarks ending in "Psych!" are not humorous; they really are cutting comments that are trying to be put off as a joke. Here's an example: "The way you are dressed you look like the rag-pickers child—*psych*—just kidding!"

ACTIVITY
Example: With your partner share a humorous story that demonstrates the concept of acceptable humor, fitting for your setting and population. Point out if there is genuine laughter without the need to "stoop" to lower standards.
Discuss: With your partner see if you can agree, in general, that sometimes humor and jokes are disrespectful and need to be eliminated. Discuss some specific examples of both types. Try not to be too serious in a discussion about humor!

Congratulations! This skill can be one of the most difficult to uphold, and there are times when the crowd will want to move forward in an unpleasant and disrespectful way, and you are the only one standing up for good manners and respect.

BIBLICAL PRINCIPLE

Humor is a gift from God designed to uplift and build camaraderie.

Proverbs 4:24 *Put away perversity from your mouth; keep corrupt talk far from your lips.*

Proverbs 11:12 *A man who lacks judgment derides his neighbor, but a man of understanding holds his tongue.*

Proverbs 12:18 *Reckless words pierce like a sword, but the tongue of the wise brings healing.*

Proverbs 16:24 (NKJV) *Pleasant words are like a honeycomb, Sweetness to the soul and health to the bones.*

Proverbs 26:18-19 *Like a madman shooting firebrands or deadly arrows is a man who deceives his neighbor and says, "I was only joking!"*

Matthew 15:10 *Jesus called the crowd to him and said, "Listen and understand. What goes into a man's mouth does not make him 'unclean', but what comes out of his mouth, that is what makes him 'unclean.'"*

Ephesians 4:29 *Do not let unwholesome talk come out of your mouths, but only what is helpful for building others up according to their needs, that it may benefit those who listen.*

James 3:9-10 *With the tongue we praise our Lord and Father, and with it we curse men, who have been made in God's likeness. Out of the same mouth come praise and cursing. My brothers, this should not be.*

MEMORY VERSE

Proverbs 17:22 *A cheerful heart is good medicine, but a crushed spirit dries up the bones.*

STUDY GUIDE

DEFINITION: Enjoying sharing humor with others, having fun in the manner of not upsetting or insulting anyone, present or absent.

Real and tasteful humor means:

_____

_____

_____

_____

_____

_____

_____

_____

"Don't" List:

1. Use obscene language
2. Refer to body parts/functions
3. Make fun or insult gender, nationality or ethnic groups

Your suggestions:

_____

_____

_____

_____

_____

_____

_____

_____

REVIEW

Humor is a gift from God designed to uplift and build camaraderie.

1. *Write :*
Proverbs 17:22 from memory on the lines below:

_____

_____

_____

_____

_____

2. *Circle the Correct Letter:*
How does Proverbs 26:18-19 describe someone who is deceitful and says, "I was only joking!"?

    a. A comedian   b. A good friend   c. A Christian   d. A madman

3. *Fill in the Blanks:*
"Pleasant words are like a honeycomb, _____ to the _____ and _____to the _____."

4. *Circle the Correct Letter:*
According to Matthew 15:10, what makes a person unclean?
    a. what comes out of his mouth
    b. going without a shower
    c. what goes into his mouth
    d. the food he eats

SKILL 2: Disagreeing Respectfully

DEFINITION: Coming from a place of different ideas, opinions, feelings and attitudes about something, yet being able to accept that you don't agree.

There are many times in life when we disagree with one or more persons. That does not necessarily mean we are unable to converse with them or enjoy each other's company.

ACTIVITY
Instructions: State your position, offer two clear, short reasons why you believe what you do, then allow a different opinion to be expressed. As a closing comment, you can respond, "I see where you are coming from, but I really can't agree with you." Maintain eye contact, open hands, a neutral or pleasant look on your face, and non-threatening posture.

Scenarios: In groups of 3–4, assign "pro" and "con" sides to the following topics:
   a. Meals should never include dessert for health reasons
   b. Everyone should belong to a union of some kind
   c. Anyone who cusses while speaking in public should be banned from the meeting
   d. If you break a rule during school you lose recess privileges
   e. Older siblings should do more chores at home

Discuss:
  (1) Times in your life when you were able to disagree and yet continue a conversation, and times when you weren't;
  (2) The necessity of being able to have people in your life with whom you are not able to agree about everything;
  (3) How, at times, value disagreements may require you not to be around someone;
  (4) How even a major difference does not mean you must take a verbal stand; the meaning and value of "picking your battles."
  (5) Situations where it may be better to excuse oneself and end the conversation.

Congratulations! You are tackling the more sensitive socialization skills and preparing for success in real life situations where you can disagree with respect.

BIBLICAL PRINCIPLE

Believers have the assurance of the infallible Word of God. God's Word is eternal and authoritative. In the midst of a disagreement, we must rest in the knowledge that God will make His way known and final (Philippians 3:15).

Psalm 141:3 *Set a guard over my mouth, O LORD; keep watch over the door of my lips.*

Proverbs 13:10 *Pride only breeds quarrels, but wisdom is found in those who take advice.*

Proverbs 15:1 *A gentle answer turns away wrath, but a harsh word stirs up anger.*

Proverbs 16:23, 32 *A wise man's heart guides his mouth, and his lips promote instruction. Better a patient man than a warrior, a man who controls his temper than one who takes a city.*

Proverbs 21:23 *He who guards his mouth and his tongue keeps himself from calamity.*

2 Timothy 2:23 (NLT) *Again I say, don't get involved in foolish, ignorant arguments that only start fights.*

Hebrews 12:14 *Make every effort to live in peace with all men and to be holy; without holiness no one will see the Lord.*

MEMORY VERSE

James 1:26 *If anyone considers himself religious and yet does not keep a tight rein on his tongue, he deceives himself and his religion is worthless.*

STUDY GUIDE

DEFINITION: Coming from a place of different ideas, opinions, feelings and attitudes about something, yet being able to accept that you don't agree.

When you disagree respectfully, you don't **(enrage, belittle, ignore)** them.

Even when you disagree, you are able to **(keep calm, agree to table the discussion until calmer, etc.).**

Sometimes you may want to **(remove yourself, agree to disagree)** rather than get into a strong disagreement.

NOTES

_____

_____

_____

_____

_____

_____

_____

_____

_____

_____

_____

REVIEW

Believers have the assurance of the infallible Word of God. God's Word is eternal and authoritative. In the midst of a disagreement, we must rest in the knowledge that God will make His way known and final.

1. *Circle the Correct Letter:*
According to Proverbs 15:1, how should you respond when another individual is expressing their anger toward you?
      a. You should respond with anger
      b. You should attempt to defend yourself
      c. You should respond with a gentle answer
      d. None of the above

2. *Fill in the Blanks:*
Philippians 3:15 teaches that _____ will make all things clear to those who are _____ in the event of a disagreement.

3. *Write :*
Titus 3:9 from memory on the lines below:

_____

_____

_____

_____

_____

_____

SKILL 3: Resolving Conflict

DEFINITION: Coming to terms with strong personal differences of beliefs and opinions with another person. (Pride and selfishness are often primary obstacles to conflict resolution.)

Not all conflict can be resolved, yet each person can have a clearer understanding of what the other believes about the topic at hand. Many times when it has been more of a spat than an intellectual disagreement, where feelings were hurt, just saying, "I am sorry for hurting your feelings, even if we can't agree" will do much to bring the conflict into a manageable size. By offering an apology, you are not saying anyone was right or wrong, but respecting the feelings of the other person. When you *are* wrong in a personal conflict, owning it and offering an apology is truly the demonstration of respect for the other party.

The goal of resolving conflict is to see where the other person is coming from by hearing their perspective. Your perspective is gained through knowing, appreciating that there is a difference, and trying to come to a place of acceptance, and if necessary, forgiveness—all done through a respectful process. Following are some ways to be respectful during a disagreement:

Monitoring your approach during this process is one of the keys to success:
    a. Volume—non-threatening
    b. Facial expressions—keep open and neutral, no looks of amazement or disgust
    c. Hand position—open, no clenched fists, no threatening or demeaning hand gestures
    d. Breathing—no sighing or snorting
    e. Eye contact—steady; no rolling of eyes
    f. Body posture—open and non-threatening

Behaviors that support success in conflict situations:
    a. Being a good listener.
    b. Speaking the truth, but not in a hurtful way
    c. Speaking with a purpose, such as coming to a resolution
    d. Articulating your ideas as clearly as possible

ACTIVITY
Practice: Privately write the name of an individual with whom you have a current unresolved conflict. Consider using the above guidelines to bring resolution and peace to the situation.
Considerations: Decide what you can and cannot agree upon, and determine what is the real issue with which you are dealing.

Congratulations! You are learning to work through some really tough social skills.

BIBLICAL PRINCIPLE

*We are identified as believers by our willingness and ability
to promote and seek peace and reconciliation.*

Proverbs 3:31 *Do not envy a violent man or choose any of his ways.*

Proverbs 10:12 *Hatred stirs up dissension, but love covers over all wrongs.*

Proverbs 12:16, 18 *A fool shows his annoyance at once, but a prudent man overlooks an insult. The words of the reckless pierce like swords, but the tongue of the wise brings healing.*

Proverbs 13:10 *Where there is strife, there is pride, but wisdom is found in those who take advice.*

Proverbs 29:11 *A fool gives full vent to his anger, but a wise man keeps himself under control.*

Ephesians 4:31-32 *Get rid of all bitterness, rage and anger, brawling and slander, along with every form of malice. Be kind and compassionate to one another, forgiving each other, just as in Christ God forgave you.*

James 1:19-20 *My dear brothers, take note of this: Everyone should be quick to listen, slow to speak and slow to become angry, for man's anger does not bring about the righteous life that God desires.*

MEMORY VERSE
Proverbs 15:1 *A gentle answer turns away wrath, but a harsh word stirs up anger.*

STUDY GUIDE

DEFINITION: Coming to terms with strong personal differences of beliefs and opinions with another person.

Pride and selfishness can be issues in conflict and can be obstacles to conflict resolution. Not all conflict can be resolved, yet each party can have a clearer understanding of what the other believes about the topic at hand. Many times when it has been more of a spat than an intellectual disagreement, where feelings were hurt, just saying "I am sorry for hurting your feelings, even if we can't agree" will do much to bring the conflict into a manageable size.

Goals of resolving conflict:

_____

_____

_____

_____

_____

Be mindful of:

       Volume

       Facial expressions

       Hand position

       Breathing

       Eye contact

       Body posture

Offer:

       Good listening

       Speak the truth without hurting

       Speak with a purpose, not just to hear yourself talk

       Present your ideas as clearly as possible

Considerations:

       Decide what you can agree on, and not agree upon.

       Determine what the real issue is that you are dealing with

REVIEW

*We are identified as believers by our willingness and ability
to promote and seek peace and reconciliation.*

1. *List:*
The behaviors stated in Ephesians 4:31-32 that we, as believers, should eliminate from our interactions with others:

_____

_____

_____

_____

_____

2. *Circle the Correct Letter:*
According to Proverbs 13:10, what sin is the source of all strife/conflict?
      a. gluttony   b. pride   c. lying   d. anger

How does Proverbs 29:11 describe someone who keeps himself under control?
      a. wise   b. foolish   c. ignorant   d. weak

3. *Write:*
Matthew 5:9 from memory on the lines below:

_____

_____

_____

_____

_____

4. *True or False:*
_____ Luke 6:28-29 instructs us to bless those who curse us and pray for those who mistreat us.

SKILL 4: Remaining Calm

DEFINITION: Staying in control of your actions, words, tone, and volume of voice when experiencing strong and usually negative emotions.

ACTIVITY

Role play: Partners can act out being scolded for losing the car keys. One party verbally attacks the other for being careless. What techniques can be shown for not losing control in this situation? You should be at a level of development for this exercise and can offer a list of responses:
    a. Taking a breath
    b. Allowing the other person to finish and then making a rational explanation
    c. Apologizing with a plan to move forward
    d. Asking to step out and have this talk when everyone is a bit cooler

Discuss: Based on past experiences, what values do you and /or group members see in this response, rather than losing control in a social situation? Share those situations when you did stay calm, and what the benefit of that was, and also when you did not, and what unwanted consequences were experienced. Discuss suggestions of how to stay calm when it would be easy not to.
Process: Process how you felt during the discussion, even those who were observers, perhaps relating to situations you did not wish to share. Close the discussion with what it looks like when cooler heads prevail and no one "feeds the storm."

Congratulations! This is a huge step forward in mastering your socialization skills. As you have noticed, the more complex ones have been left until you gained a foundation on which to build.

BIBLICAL PRINCIPLE

Believers must demonstrate soberness in their approach to life by not allowing their emotions to master them or dictate their behavior.

Proverbs 12:16 *A fool shows his annoyance at once, but a prudent man overlooks an insult.*

Proverbs 14:17 *A quick-tempered man does foolish things, and a crafty man is hated.*

Proverbs 25:28 *Like a city whose walls are broken down is a man who lacks self-control.*

Galatians 5:22-23 *But the fruit of the Spirit is love, joy, peace, patience, kindness, goodness, faithfulness, gentleness, and self-control. Against such things there is no law.*

Philippians 4:6 *Do not be anxious about anything, but in everything, by prayer and petition, with thanksgiving, present your requests to God.*

2 Timothy 1:7 *For God did not give us a spirit of timidity, but a spirit of power, of love and of self-discipline.*

1 Peter 1:13 *Therefore, prepare your minds for action, be self-controlled; set your hope fully on the grace to be given you when Jesus Christ is revealed.*

1 Peter 5:8 *Be self-controlled and alert. Your enemy the devil prowls around like a roaring lion looking for someone to devour.*

MEMORY VERSE

Proverbs 29:11 *A fool gives full vent to his anger, but a wise man keeps himself under control.*

STUDY GUIDE

DEFINITION: Staying in control of your actions, words, tone and volume of voice when experiencing strong and negative emotions.

1. Discuss why staying calm can be better for you:

_____

_____

_____

_____

_____

_____

2. Discuss when in past situations you have lost your "calm" and wished you hadn't:

_____

_____

_____

_____

_____

_____

<u>REVIEW</u>

Believers must demonstrate soberness in their approach to life by not allowing their emotions to master them or dictate their behavior.

1. *List :*
The fruit of the Spirit found in Galatians 5:22-23:

_____

_____

_____

_____

2. *Circle the Correct Letter:*
Proverbs 29:11 describes someone who does not keep his emotions under control as a:

    a. genius   b. fool   c. lawyer   d. hero

3. *True or False:*
_____Being self-controlled and alert protects us against our enemy, the devil, who prowls around looking for someone to devour.

4. *Fill in the Blanks:*
"For God did not give us a spirit of _____ but a spirit of _____ of _____ and of _____."

2 Timothy 1:7

III

Humility

SKILL 1: Introducing Self and Others

DEFINITION: Telling someone who you are, shaking their hand and looking them in the eye while you are speaking and when they are speaking to you.

ACTIVITY
1. **Practice:** Stand up, approach another person in the room, and do the following: • Look them directly in the eye. • Have a pleasant look on your face. • Extend your hand. • Say, "I am _____, and I am glad to meet you." • Listen when they reply with their name, looking them in the eye while shaking their hand. • Give a firm, yet never hurtful, handshake. • Thank them and then choose whether to exchange words in a conversation or end the exchange.
2. **Homework:** Place yourself in a casual, real life situation where there is someone you don't know but with whom you might have a reason to strike up a conversation. Follow each of the above steps.
3. **Analyze:** Discuss the thoughts and feelings you had as you compare the controlled classroom scenario with your real life experience.

Congratulations! You are more prepared to put yourself and others at ease when you first meet.

BIBLICAL PRINCIPLE

*Setting a tone of peace and wellness enables the believer
to establish a godly witness and trust within a relationship;
thus providing an opportunity for sharing his/her faith.*

Genesis 18:1-5 *The Lord appeared to Abraham near the great trees of Mamre while he was sitting at the entrance to his tent in the heat of the day. Abraham looked up and saw three men standing nearby. When he saw them, he hurried from the entrance of his tent to meet them and bowed low to the ground.*

Genesis 43:29 *As he looked about and saw his brother Benjamin, his own mother's son, he asked, "Is this your youngest brother, the one you told me about?" And he said, "God be gracious to you, my son."*

1 Samuel 25:5-6 *So he sent ten young men and said to them, "Go up to Nabal at Carmel and greet him in my name. Say to him: Long life to you! Good health to you and your household! And good health to all that is yours!"*

Matthew 10:11-13 *Whatever town or village you enter, search there for some worthy person and stay at their house until you leave. As you enter the home, give it your greeting. If the home is deserving, let your peace rest on it; if it is not, let your peace return to you.*

Luke 1:40-41, 44 *She entered Zechariah's home and greeted Elizabeth. When Elizabeth heard Mary's greeting, the baby leaped in her womb, and Elizabeth was filled with the Holy Spirit. As soon as the sound of your greeting reached my ears, the baby in my womb leaped for joy.*

1 Corinthians 16:19-20 *The churches in the province of Asia send you greetings. Aquila and Priscilla greet you warmly in the Lord, and so does the church that meets at their house. All the brothers here send you greetings. Greet one another with a holy kiss.*

MEMORY VERSE
1 Peter 5:14 *Greet one another with a kiss of love. Peace to all of you who are in Christ.*

STUDY GUIDE

DEFINITION: Telling someone who you are, shaking their hand and looking them in the eye while you are speaking and when they are speaking to you.

1. After your discussion with your partner or the group, prepare a general personal greeting and write it on the lines below. Be sure to include some of the characteristics discussed in group.

   _____

   _____

   _____

   _____

   _____

   _____

   _____

2. Circle all of the positive characteristics found in David's response to Abigail's greeting in 1 Samuel 25:32-33, 35 below:

   David said to Abigail, "Praise be to the LORD, the God of Israel, who has sent you today to meet me. May you be blessed for your good judgment and for keeping me from bloodshed this day and from avenging myself with my own hand. Then David accepted from her hand what she had brought him and said, "Go home in peace, I have heard your words and granted your request."

3. Write: 1 Peter 5:14 on the lines below.

   _____

   _____

   _____

   _____

4. Describe what types of physical contact are appropriate upon greetings and introductions:

_____

_____

_____

_____

_____

_____

_____

_____

_____

_____

_____

_____

REVIEW

Setting a tone of peace and wellness enables the believer to establish a godly witness and trust within a relationship, thus providing an opportunity for sharing his/her faith.

1. *Circle the Correct Letter:*

Read 1 Samuel 25:5-6. What three blessings did David wish for Nabal in his greeting?
   a. Long life, health to him and his household, and health to everything that belongs to him
   b. Financial security, good relationships, and love
   c. Wisdom, love, and faith
   d. Winning the Lotto, fame and fortune, and happiness

According to Matthew 10:11-13, what should you do upon entering a home and what should rest upon the home during your stay:
   a. Turn on the TV (your feet)
   b. Greet the hosts (your peace)
   c. Demand a meal (chaos)
   d. Make a phone call (turmoil)

2. *List :*
The three (3) positive characteristics of a greeting:

_____

_____

_____

_____

_____

SKILL 2: Living With Good Manners

DEFINITION: Way of behaving with other's welfare being regarded above self.

When living in a social world, with, and around other people, there is a need for personal interactions that allow for and support having a respectful process. That process is good manners.

Discuss here what is understood by good manners, and what value you see in demonstrating them with other people—and perhaps how that had not been a strong characteristic in your past.

Due to the widespread use of cell phones and hand-held games, it is necessary to include a section on the correct and appropriate use of them. When preoccupied with using these items, you can have complete disregard for those around you, thus not exhibiting good manners.

Talking on a cell phone is a private activity and needs to be conducted out of hearing range of others. That means talking on the phone while being with people is not showing good manners. If the conversation is necessary and cannot be held at a later time, excuse yourself from the other person's company and conduct your conversation, keeping your voice to a volume that does not disturb others. This means that speaking on the phone or texting is to be done in private, and not done half in and half out of being with other people.

Think about how rude it is to both parties – those on the phone, wanting your attention, and those with you, wanting your attention. The same considerations need to be in place with regard to hand-held games. Being focused on the company in front of you is key to demonstrating good manners and being that social person who wants to be successful in society.

ACTIVITY
Scene 1: Practice holding the door for someone behind you. Then trade places.
Scene 2: Pretend you are at the dinner table. Using eye contact, ask for something to be passed to you. Say "please" when making the request, and "thank you" when it is given. Trade places.
Scene 3: Ask a question of a female you don't know, beginning with "Ma'am" and closing with "thank you." Now ask a question of a male you don't know, begin with "Sir", close with "thank you."

Scene 4: Pretend you are at a dinner table when you receive a call on your cell phone because you didn't have it turned off. What would acting rudely look like, and what would using good manners look like?

Congratulations! You are building your skills for a more effective life in your society. When you conduct yourself with good manners while with other people, you are demonstrating respect for yourself and for them.

BIBLICAL PRINCIPLE

*To treat others with respect, love, kindness and
hospitality is the sacred duty of the believer.*

Leviticus 19:33 *When a foreigner resides among you in your land, do not mistreat them. The foreigner residing among you must be treated as your native-born. Love them as yourself, for you were foreigners in Egypt. I am the LORD your God.*

Romans 12:13 *Share with the Lord's people who are in need. Practice hospitality.*

Colossians 3:12 *Therefore, as God's chosen people, holy and dearly loved, clothe yourselves with compassion, kindness, humility, gentleness and patience.*

Hebrews 13:2 *Do not forget to entertain strangers, for by so doing some people have entertained angels without knowing it.*

1 Peter 4:9-11 *Offer hospitality to one another without grumbling. Each one should use whatever gift he has received to serve others, faithfully administering God's grace in its various forms. If anyone speaks, he should do it as one speaking the very words of God. If anyone serves, he should do it with the strength God provides, so that in all things God may be praised through Jesus Christ. To him be the glory and the power for ever and ever. Amen.*

MEMORY VERSE

James 2:8 *If you really keep the royal law found in Scripture, "Love your neighbor as you love yourself," you are doing right.*

DEFINITION: Way of behaving with other's welfare being regarded above self.

STUDY GUIDE

Fill in the acrostic. Verses are found in Genesis 18:1-8.

WORD	VERSE
M – meet-meal	_____
A –accept-acknowledge	_____
N - noble	_____
N - notable	_____
E – extra mile	_____
R - respect	_____
S – servant heart	_____

Select a behavior from the acrostic above that you would like to improve upon and implement in your own social interactions. Describe how you plan to implement the behavior.

_____

_____

_____

_____

_____

Write Matthew 7:12 on the lines and memorize the verse:

_____

_____

_____

_____

<u>REVIEW</u>

*The sacred duty of the believer is to treat others
with respect, love, kindness, and hospitality.*

1. *List:*
The desired believer's characteristics according to Colossians:

_____

_____

_____

_____

_____

2. *Write:*
Matthew 7:12 from memory on the lines below:

_____

_____

_____

_____

_____

3. *Review*:
Genesis 18:1-8. Match the acrostic letters for
MANNERS
with the correct verses:

3. *Fill in the Blank:*
Hebrews 13:2 states that by entertaining strangers we might unknowingly entertain

_____.

SKILL 3: Showing Respect

DEFINITION: Manner of acting toward another person that reflects your valuing them as an individual.

Showing respect to another person(s) is an integral and key part of living successfully in any society. All of the skills to this point are part of showing respect through your behavior. The simple tasks of making eye contact, listening, introducing yourself and having good manners are essential steps in showing respect.

Showing respect to others reflects the respect that you have for yourself. As you move forward in developing and refining your socialization skills, there are behaviors that need to be included with the basic ones mentioned above.

This can be a time for discussion of showing respect, how it is demonstrated, and when society believes is it necessary.

Following are several suggested scenarios where this skill can be applied. Ask the group to name others and discuss the expected behavior:

- When "The Star Spangled Banner" is played during a public event.
- When a public event is starting (e.g. church, movie, speech, etc.).
- When approaching others who are engaged in conversation.

ACTIVITY
Scene 1. With a partner begin a conversation, and then one of you turn away and begin speaking to another person who is nearby. Trade places until each one has been both abandoned and has done the abandoning.
Scene 2. In your partnership/group assign someone to lead a discussion, then have someone else start talking and laughing loudly with a person nearby. Trade roles until each one has been a leader and has been disruptive.
Scene 3. Two participants begin a conversation with one another, and then have a third person enter into the conversation, interrupting and speaking over everyone. Trade roles until each person has been interrupted and has done the interrupting.
Discuss: Describe what you thought and felt during each role in each scene. Did you become angry or irritated at any point? Did you feel ashamed or self-conscious at any point?

Congratulations! You are developing a more sensitive understanding of respect.

BIBLICAL PRINCIPLE

Christians must be "others-focused" and humble.

Leviticus 19:32 *Stand up in the presence of the aged, show respect for the elderly and revere your God. I am the LORD.*

Luke 14:7-11 *When he noticed how the guests picked the places of honor at the table, he told them this parable: "When someone invites you to a wedding feast, do not take the place of honor, for a person more distinguished than you may have been invited. If so, the host who invited both of you will come and say to you, 'Give this person your seat.' Then, humiliated, you will have to take the least important place. But when you are invited, take the lowest place, so that when your host comes, he will say to you, 'Friend, move up to a better place.' Then you will be honored in the presence of all the other guests. For all those who exalt themselves will be humbled, and those who humble themselves will be exalted."*

Romans 12:10 *Be devoted to one another in love. Honor one another above yourselves.*

Romans 13:7 *Give everyone what you owe him: If you owe taxes, pay taxes; if revenue, then revenue; if respect, then respect; if honor, then honor.*

Ephesians 6:2-3 *"Honor your father and mother"—which is the first commandment with a promise—"that it may go well with you and that you may enjoy long life on the earth."*

1 Peter 2:17 *Show proper respect to everyone: Love the brotherhood of believers, fear God, honor the king.*

MEMORY VERSE

Philippians 2:3 *Do nothing out of selfish ambition or vain conceit, but in humility consider others better than yourselves.*

STUDY GUIDE

DEFINITION: Manner of acting toward another person that reflects your valuing them as an individual.

After thoughtful consideration, answer the following questions.

1. Can you remember one situation in the past that stands out when you regretted not showing respect? Describe here.

_____

_____

_____

_____

_____

_____

_____

_____

_____

2. Re-assess the situation and your response from where you are now. What would you do differently? And why.

_____

_____

_____

_____

_____

_____

_____

_____

_____

REVIEW

Christians must be 'others focused' and humble.

1. *Fill in the Blanks:*
Read Leviticus 19:32 and Ephesians 6:2-3. What two groups of people are we commanded to show honor and respect to?

_____ and _____

2. *Circle the Correct Letter:*
According to Leviticus 19:32, what is one example of demonstrating respect to the elderly.
   a. Turning your back to them
   b. Waving hello from your seat
   c. Applauding their presence
   d. Standing up in their presence

3. *Write:*
Philippians 2:3 from memory on the lines below:

_____

_____

_____

4. *True or False:*

_____ According to Ephesians 6:3, honoring your father and mother will promise to result in a long and prosperous life.

IV

Relationships

SKILL 1: Reading Emotions

DEFINITION: Being able to correctly identify what emotions another person is feeling.

Success in this skill can be related to how effectively you are able to identify your own emotions. Do you know when you are really angry, fearful or sad? Many times fear comes out like anger, and selfishness does as well. Is it anger, and if it is, what are you feeling combative about? Sorting out these differences in yourself is the beginning of being able to identify them in others.

ACTIVITY

Role play: In your partnership/group, have different members silently posture specific feelings and have the others identify the correct feeling. Use body language to help demonstrate the feeling being postured. Add other feelings as time and creativity allow.
    a. Anger
    b. Happiness
    c. Sadness

Group Leader: Use a personal example from driving in which you were afraid of being hit and in your confusion reacted angrily. Recall an example when a child ran into a dangerous spot and an adult's fear looked like anger.
Share: Ask for sharing from the group/partner. Have you masked your feelings so successfully that there is confusion about the real ones?
Discuss: What is the value of this social skill? What is the importance of being able to correctly identify and then respond appropriately to another's emotions?

Congratulations! At this moment, however, you probably have no idea how huge this skill is in being effective in socializing or in personal relationships!

BIBLICAL PRINCIPLE

*Believers must exercise discernment to determine the
emotional needs of an individual and minister accordingly.*

Psalm 42:5 *Why are you downcast, O my soul? Why so disturbed within me? Put your hope in God, for I will yet praise him, my Savior and my God.*

Psalm 55:22 *Cast your cares on the LORD and he will sustain you; he will never let the righteous fall.*

Proverbs 12:25 *An anxious heart weighs a man down, but a kind word cheers him up.*

Proverbs 15:13 *A happy heart makes the face cheerful, but heartache crushes the spirit.*

Matthew 5:4 *Blessed are those who mourn, for they will be comforted.*

Matthew 11:28 *Come to me, all you who are weary and burdened, and I will give you rest.*

Romans 12:1 *Rejoice with those who rejoice; mourn with those who mourn.*

Galatians 6:2 *Carry each other's burdens, and in this way you will fulfill the law of Christ.*

Ephesians 4:32 *Be kind and compassionate to one another, forgiving each other, just as in Christ God forgave you.*

Philippians 4:6-7 *Do not be anxious about anything, but in everything, by prayer and petition, with thanksgiving, present your requests to God. And the peace of God, which transcends all understanding, will guard your hearts and your minds in Christ Jesus.*

Hebrews 3:13 *But encourage one another daily, as long as it is called Today, so that none of you may be hardened by sin's deceitfulness.*

MEMORY VERSE

2 Corinthians 1:3-4 *Praise be to the God and Father of our Lord Jesus Christ, the Father or compassion and the God of all comfort, who comforts us in all our troubles, so that we can comfort those in any trouble with the comfort we ourselves have received from God.*

<u>STUDY GUIDE</u>

DEFINITION: Being able to correctly identify what emotions another person is feeling.

Success in this skill can be related to how effectively you can identify your own emotions.

Do you know when you are really angry, fearful, or sad? Many times fear comes out like anger, and selfishness does as well. Is it anger, and if it is, what are you feeling combative about: Sorting out these differences in yourself is the beginning of being able to identify them in others.

Angry feels, sounds, and looks like:

_____

_____

_____

_____

_____

Happy feels, sounds, and looks like:

_____

_____

_____

_____

_____

Sad feels, sounds, and looks like:

_____

_____

_____

_____

_____

REVIEW

*Believers must exercise discernment to determine the emotional needs
of an individual and minister accordingly.*

1. *Circle the Correct Letter:*
According to 2 Corinthians 1:3-4, how can you use the comfort you receive from God
during our own troubles?
   a. You can journal your feelings
   b. You can ignore the needs of others
   c. You can pray for them
   d. You can comfort those in trouble

2. *Fill in the Blank:*
Hebrews 3:13 instructs us to _____ one another daily.

3. *Discuss:*
According to Proverbs 12:25, how can you cheer someone up who is anxious?

4. *True or False:*
_____4. Romans 12:1 tells us to rejoice with those who mourn and mourn
with those who rejoice.

SKILL 2: Persuading Others

DEFINITION: Bringing someone else to accept and agree with what you think, believe, feel, or have an opinion about.

The art of bringing someone else to this position of acceptance is a complicated one. Sometimes people will accept a position because you know more about the subject than they do. Sometimes they will adopt your position because they don't really have a position of their own, and sometimes just because they like you. On the other side, there are the times when they won't agree with you just because they don't like you.

Knowing when it is important to persuade someone, and knowing how far to go in that pursuit, calls for maturity and self-discipline. Following are some suggestions:

1. Know what you want to persuade them about in your own mind-**P**URPOSE
2. Know what you are talking about-**P**REPARATION
3. Have at least three valid reasons why you think they should come to your position-**P**ERSUASION
4. Be able to show them the benefit of agreeing with you-**P**OISE
5. Be willing to accept that it may not happen, at least the way you want it to-**P**EACE

ACTIVITY
Scenario 1: Have one partnership/group member attempt to talk another out of his last dollar. Switch sides. Try alternatives of giving in and not giving in.
Scenario 2: In your partnership/ group have a participant agree to be persuaded (with some effort) about something and then demonstrate how that sounds.
Discuss: Share when someone tried unsuccessfully to persuade you of something and it didn't work. Then share a time when you were persuaded. Can you determine what made the difference? If anyone has sales or team experience, ask them to share how they were instructed to persuade others.

Congratulations! You have just worked your way through another tough social skill that was built on the other skills. You have seen what respect can look like when you want something from someone, and they from you. This skill takes much thoughtful practice.

<u>BIBLICAL PRINCIPLE</u>

*Believers must be prepared to persuade people to respond positively to
the Scripture's message of grace and calling to commit their life to Christ.*

Proverbs 9:9 *Instruct a wise man and he will be wiser still; teach a righteous man and he will add to his learning.*

Proverbs 18:21 (NKJV) *Death and life are in the power of the tongue, And those who love it will eat its fruit.*

Matthew 7:28 *When Jesus had finished saying these things, the crowds were amazed at his teaching, because he taught as one who had authority, and not as their teachers of the law.*

Matthew 28:19 *Therefore, go and make disciples of all nations, baptizing them in the name of the Father and of the Son and of the Holy Spirit, and teaching them to obey everything I have commanded you. And surely I am with you always, to the very end of the age.*

Mark 13:9-11 *You must be on your guard. You will be handed over to the local councils and flogged in the synagogues. On account of me you will stand before governors and kings as witnesses to them. And the gospel must first be preached to all nations. Whenever you are arrested and brought to trial, do not worry beforehand about what to say. Just say whatever is given you at the time, for it is not you speaking, but the Holy Spirit.*

Acts 13:47-48 *For this is what the Lord has commanded us: "I have made you a light for the Gentiles, that you may bring salvation to the ends of the earth." When the Gentiles heard this, they were glad and honored the word of the Lord; and all who were appointed for eternal life believed.*

<u>MEMORY VERSE</u>
1 Peter 3:15-16 *But in your hearts set apart Christ as Lord. Always be prepared to give an answer to everyone who asks you to give the reason for the hope that you have. But do this with gentleness and respect, keeping a clear conscience, so that those who speak maliciously against your good behavior in Christ may be ashamed of their slander.*

STUDY GUIDE

DEFINITION : Bringing someone else to accept and agree with what you think, believe, feel, or have an opinion about.

1. List the *Five P's of Persuasion*:

    1. _____

    2. _____

    3. _____

    4. _____

    5. _____

2. What is our primary purpose, as believers, for acquiring the skill of Persuading Others?

    _____

    _____

    _____

3. *Fill in the Blanks:*

1 Peter 3: 15-16 instructs us to be _____ and _____ when explaining to others the reason for the hope we have in Christ.

4. State your purpose for trying to bring someone to the Lord: _____

    _____

    _____

    _____

    _____

    _____

    _____

5. What are you going to share about? What are the facts?

_____

_____

_____

_____

_____

_____

_____

6. Give at least 3 reasons why you think they should come to accept Christ as their Savior.

_____

_____

_____

_____

_____

7. How would you open your discussion?

_____

_____

_____

_____

8. How would you close your discussion?

_____

_____

_____

_____

9. How will you respond if they reject your invitation for salvation?

_____

_____

_____

_____

_____

_____

_____

_____

_____

_____

_____

_____

_____

_____

_____

_____

_____

_____

_____

_____

_____

_____

_____

_____

_____

REVIEW

Believers must be prepared to persuade people to respond positively to the Scripture's message of grace and calling to commit their life to Christ.

1. *Circle the Correct Letter:*

Matthew 28:19 commands us to:
   a. Make disciples, baptize others, teach obedience
   b. Make friends, socialize often, relax
   c. Read the Bible, pray for others, be helpful
   d. All of the above

2. *Fill in the Blanks:*

According to Proverbs 18:21, our words have the power to bring _____ or _____ others.

1 Peter 3:15-16 instructs us to be _____ and _____ when explaining to others the reason for the hope we have in Christ.
   a. firm and authoritative
   b. open-minded and agreeable
   c. argumentative and disagreeable
   d. none of the above

3. *True or False:*

_____. According to Matthew 7:28, the crowds were amazed at Jesus' teachings because he spoke as one who had authority.

SKILL 3: Demonstrating Appropriate Affection during Conversations

DEFINITION: Demonstrating fondness in a respectful manner, without upsetting the recipients.

Sometimes there can be confusion as to what is acceptable during conversation when you want to show someone fondness or comfortableness. This can be confusing for both of you, whether the other person is of the same gender or not. Some people talk with their hands and just naturally seem to reach out to other people while in conversation.

When in conversation, it is acceptable most of the time to touch another person from the wrist up to the shoulder. When sitting, it is never advisable to touch another person anywhere on their leg.

When giving hugs, the "A-frame" hug is least personal and still allows for exchanging a sign of greeting or affection.

ACTIVITY
Demonstrate: Ask for a volunteer and demonstrate acceptable hugs and contact during both sitting and standing conversations or greetings.
Discuss: Volunteer to share your experiences of when you were both comfortable and uncomfortable with hugs and other types of affectionate public greetings.

Congratulations! You have just added a social skill that will keep the people in your presence comfortable and feeling respected by you and your respectful signs of affection.

BIBLICAL PRINCIPLE

Believers would be wise to apply healthy boundaries during personal interactions with others in order to guard against temptations and misunderstandings.

1 Thessalonians 4:3-7 *It is God's will that you should be sanctified: That you should avoid sexual immorality; that each of you should learn to control his own body in a way that is holy and honorable, not in passionate lust like the heathen, who do not know God; and that in this matter no one should wrong his brother or take advantage of him. The Lord will punish men for all such sins, as we have already told you and warned you. For God did not call us to be impure, but to live a holy life.*

Psalm 139:23-24 *Search me, O God, and know my heart; test me and know my anxious thoughts. See if there is any offensive way in me, and lead me in the way everlasting.*

Romans 15:1 *We who are strong ought to bear with the failings of the weak and not to please ourselves.*

Philippians 2:3-4 *Do nothing out of selfish ambition or vain conceit, but in humility consider others better than yourselves. Each of you should look not only to your own interests, but also to the interests of others.*

Matthew 5:8 *Blessed are the pure in heart, for they will see God.*

1 Corinthians 10:13 *No temptation has seized you except what is common to man. And God is faithful; he will not let you be tempted beyond what you can bear. But when you are tempted, he will also provide a way out so that you can stand up under it.*

MEMORY VERSE

1 Corinthians 13:4-7 *Love is patient, love is kind. It does not envy, it does not boast, it is not proud. It is not rude, it is not self-seeking, it is not easily angered, it keeps no record of wrongs. Love does not delight in evil but rejoices with the truth. It always protects, always trusts, always hopes, always perseveres.*

<u>STUDY GUIDE</u>

DEFINITION: Demonstrating fondness in a respectful manner, without upsetting the recipients.

It can be confusing as to what is acceptable when you want to show someone while talking to them that you care for them. Or do you just talk with your hands moving? In either case, boundaries are necessary.

Thoughtfully consider what are acceptable boundaries for touching when in conversation, and why.

1. When speaking with a female, if you are male, what physical boundaries are to be honored, and why.

   _____

   _____

   _____

   _____

   _____

   _____

2. What boundaries do you expect, want, from those in conversation with you, and why.

   _____

   _____

   _____

   _____

   _____

   _____

   _____

   _____

REVIEW

Believers would be wise to apply healthy boundaries during personal interactions with others in order to guard against temptations and misunderstandings.

1. *Circle the Correct Letter:*
According to 1 Thessalonians 4:3-7, how can we avoid wronging or taking advantage of others while interacting in a social relationship or setting?
   a. Behaving in a manner that is holy and honorable
   b. Avoiding others
   c. Behaving in a manner that is rude and obnoxious
   d. B and C

2. *Discuss:*
What is the promise for the pure in heart, stated in Matthew 5:8?

_____

_____

_____

_____

_____

_____

3. *List:*
The five characteristics of **love** found in 1 Corinthians 13:4-7:

_____

_____

_____

_____

_____

_____

_____

_____

_____

_____

_____

Establish

effective

social

skills

that

work

SECTION TWO

Critical Thinking Skills

with **Biblical Principles**

Liken & Associates

Introduction

What is Critical Thinking?

DEFINITION: Taking charge of your own thinking through a disciplined process. It includes analyzing and investigating a more rational life-directing process, not based on emotions.

Introduction to Biblical Principles

As believers, we must align our thoughts, opinions and perceptions with the principles and teachings of the word of God.

Isaiah 55:9 *As the heavens are higher than the earth, so are my ways higher than your ways and my thoughts than your thoughts.*

Psalm 119:73 *Your hands made me and formed me; give me understanding to learn your commands.*

Proverbs 4:13 *Hold on to instruction, do not let it go; guard it well, for it is your life.*

1 Corinthians 2:15-16 *The spiritual man makes judgments about all things, but he [God] himself is not subject to any man's judgment: For who has known the mind of the Lord that he may instruct him? But we have the mind of Christ.*

2 Corinthians 10:5 *We demolish arguments and every pretension that sets itself up against the knowledge of God, and we take captive every thought to make it obedient to Christ.*

Ephesians 4:22-24 *You were taught, with regard to your former way of life, to put off your old self, which is being corrupted by its deceitful desires; to be made new in the attitude of your minds; and to put on the new self, created to be like God in true righteousness and holiness.*

1 Peter 4:1-3 *Therefore, since Christ suffered in his body, arm yourselves also with the same attitude, because he who has suffered in his body is done with sin. As a result, he does not live the rest of his earthly life for evil human desires, but rather for the will of God. For you have spent enough time in the past doing what pagans choose to do—living in debauchery, lust, drunkenness, orgies, carousing and detestable idolatry.*

Philippians 2:4-6 *Each of you should look not only to your own interests, but also to the interests of others. Your attitude should be the same as that of Christ Jesus: Who, being in very nature God, did not consider equality with God something to be grasped. A humble heart is foundational for developing the right attitude and outlook for life.*

V

Wisdom

SKILL 1: Adopting and Demonstrating a Positive Attitude

DEFINITION: Choosing a manner of acting, feeling, thinking, and speaking that shows one's disposition . . . opinion, mental set, a positive attitude that focuses on the glass half full.

One way to demonstrate and encourage your own positive attitude is to change your vocabulary. Positive words support a positive attitude.

> Negative: "Today it is raining. I hate rain."
> Positive: "Today it is raining, and the grass really needs it."

Can Do / Want To vs. Have To Attitudes

How do you approach something that you want to do? Now compare that to how you feel when you HAVE TO do something. When you believe that you "have to" do things, is your attitude toward doing them negative? When you convert that to a "want to" attitude, does it feel different and is the end result different?

> Have-To: "I have to go to work."
> Want-To: "I want to pay my rent and be responsible, so I want to go to work to earn the money for the rent."

Changing Vocabulary

What you say reflects what you think and underscores what you feel. Are you aware of how you state your thoughts? Do you use negative, angry words, rather than positive or neutral words?

> Negative: The food is nasty and I hate eating it.

ACTIVITY
1. With a partner rephrase the above sentence so that it can have the same message, that you are not crazy about the food, yet not in such a negative way.
2. On the Note pages write one "Have To" attitude. Re-write it as a "Want To" attitude. With a partner or in the group discuss the difference in how it sounds and how that change can help to move you forward to where you want to be.

Congratulations! You have begun the shift in thinking that leads to moving forward on your journey to where and how you want to be.

BIBLICAL PRINCIPLE

*God has dominion and control over every
situation, circumstance, or event in our lives.*

Joshua 1:9 *Have I not commanded you? Be strong and courageous. Do not be terrified; do not be discouraged, for the LORD your God will be with you wherever you go.*

Proverbs 15:13 *A happy heart makes the face cheerful, but heartache crushes the spirit.*

Proverbs 15:15 *All the days of the oppressed are wretched, but the cheerful heart has a continual feast.*

John 16:33 *I have told you these things, so that in me you may have peace. In this world you will have trouble. But take heart! I have overcome the world.*

2 Corinthians 9:8 *And God is able to make all grace abound to you, so that in all things at all times, having all that you need, you will abound in every good work.*

Philippians 4:11-13 *I am not saying this because I am in need, for I have learned to be content whatever he circumstances. I know what it is to be in need, and I know what it is to have plenty. I have learned the secret of being content in any and every situation, whether well fed or hungry, whether living in plenty or in want. I can do everything through him who gives me strength.*

Hebrews 10:23 *Let us hold unswervingly to the hope we profess, for he who promised is faithful.*

James 1:2-4 *Consider it pure joy, my brothers, whenever you face trials of many kinds, because you know that the testing of your faith develops perseverance. Perseverance must finish its work so that you may be mature and complete, not lacking anything.*

MEMORY VERSE

Romans 8:28 *And we know that in all things God works for the good of those who love him, who have been called according to his purpose.*

<u>STUDY GUIDE</u>

DEFINITION: Taking the position that the glass is ½ full, or can be.

When life is seen as "doable," there is a change in attitude. Knowing that thoughts, attitudes, and feelings drive behavior, is it easier to see why what happens in our minds determines the rest of what happens in our lives.

One way to influence attitude is by thinking and speaking in positive words and phrases. No joke, it can work.

Consider what you know about being positive and answer the following questions.

1. Think of one task in front of you about which you are procrastinating . . . write it down as it is in your mind now:

   _____

   _____

   _____

   _____

   _____

   _____

2. Now, reword it so that it reads in a positive way:

   _____

   _____

   _____

   _____

   _____

   _____

   _____

   _____

<u>REVIEW</u>

As Christ encouraged, enlightened and edified his listeners, His positive attitude shone through his every thought, feeling and action.

1. *Fill in the Blanks:*
According to Proverbs 15:13, *A happy heart makes the* _____ *cheerful, but heartache crushes the* _____ *.*

One way to influence attitude is to _____ and _____ in positive phrases.

2. *Discuss:*
What is the promise made in **Hebrews 10:23.**

_____

_____

_____

_____

3. *Fill in the Blank:*
Let us hold unswervingly to the hope we profess, for He who promised is _____ *.*
      a. unworthy   b. apt to change His mind   c. faithful

SKILL 2: Setting Attainable Goals

DEFINITION: Deciding what you want, where you want to be, or what you want to accomplish.

Goals and goal setting serve as a starting point for moving forward with critical thinking skills. Some of the words best describing goals are: aims, ambitions, aspirations, ends, objectives, purposes, results, and targets.

Another type of goal is a desired outcome of an action. The goal can serve as motivation when it is wanted and the goal setter strives to achieve it. Decision-making is key to goal setting. If the goal is specific, and has a time limit, it usually is more effective and achievable.

The goal setting process looks like this:

- **Choose** a goal
- **Set** the goal
- **Develop** an action plan to meet the goal
- **Measure** the success or failure of meeting the goal in order to adjust the plan or path for the next time

How do you develop clear and specific goals? When you follow a thoughtful process, it is more likely that the goal will be achieved.

- Write the goal with an action verb, with _to_ in front of it
- Set the time frame of completion
- Include a measurement
- Review the results, evaluate, and adjust for the next time

ACTIVITY
Choose: Make a list of goals and then choose one that you deem the most achievable in one week's time. Write, "My goal is to____."
Set: As a group/partnership commit to achieving the goal.
Develop: Formulate a plan of action to meet the selected goal.
Measure: Plan to report back after a week on the progress of the plan and goal.

Congratulations! You are more aware of the power of setting goals and have a model for doing it.

BIBLICAL PRINCIPLE

Worthwhile goals have eternal value, require perseverance, and are best determined through a fervent search of God's individual will for our lives through prayer, godly counsel, and a study of the Scriptures.

Psalm 25:9 *He guides the humble in what is right and teaches them his way.*

Psalm 32:8 *I will instruct you and teach you in the way you should go; I will counsel you and watch over you.*

Psalm 37:23 *If the LORD delights in a man's way, he makes his steps firm.*

Proverbs 2:6, 8-9 *For the LORD gives wisdom, and from his mouth come knowledge and understanding. (8) ...for he guards the course of the just and protects the way of his faithful ones. (9) Then you will understand what is right and just and fair – every good path.*

Proverbs 16:9 *In his heart a man plans his course, but the LORD determines his steps.*

Jeremiah 10:23 *I know, O LORD, that a man's life is not his own; it is not for man to direct his steps.*

Romans 12:2 *Do not conform any longer to the pattern of this world, but be transformed by the renewing of your mind. Then you will be able to test and approve what God's will is-his good, pleasing and perfect will.*

2 Thessalonians 3:5 *May the Lord direct your hearts into God's love and Christ's perseverance.*

James 1:5 *If any of you lacks wisdom, he should ask God, who gives generously to all without finding fault, and it will be given to him.*

MEMORY VERSE

Philippians 3:14 *I press on toward the goal to win the prize for which God has called me heavenward in Christ Jesus.*

STUDY GUIDE

DEFINITION: Deciding where you want to head, and choosing what outcome is desirable.

Setting goals means that you have decided where you want to go, how you will get there, and who you will be when you arrive.

Many years can be wasted in a **L**ife of **D**rifting **A**long, never making a plan, ending up nowhere that you had planned, and really wondering just how that happened. In order to look back on your life and see that you did get to where you wanted to be, you must decide where that is . . . and further, what will you be doing when you get there. In order for that to become real, you must set those goals, and then design the plan for the journey.

There are short-term goals and long-term goals. Each is important and necessary. Examples of short-term goals are to "read a book in the next 30 days," "organize my papers in the next seven days," "attend x-number of meetings in 10 days," and so on.

Long-term goals can be anywhere from six months to 5–10 years. All goals require planning, review, and then perhaps re-adjusting.

Just as important as the goal is the timeline for accomplishing it. You can have well constructed and well meaning goals set, yet without timelines, you can "drift" and never get there.

Look at the significant areas of your life. For each area, write one simple, short-term goal, and then decide on a rational timeline by which to meet it.

Personal: _____ Date: _____

Family/Friends: _____ Date: _____

Financial: _____ Date: _____

Career/Job/School/Training: _____ Date: _____

Spiritual: _____ Date: _____

In order to follow through, choose an accountability partner with whom to discuss your goals and timelines, and then report back to them on or before those dates with your outcomes.

OPTIONAL REVIEW FOR GOAL SETTING

1. Goals can be defined as :
    a._____the choice wanted, regardless of risk, even going against Biblical principles
    b._____the results of sound and effective decision making
    c._____what your friends want for you
    d._____all of the above

2. Having goals is appropriate for:
    a._____children in grade school
    b._____stay at home and/or career moms
    c._____people wanting to move forward to where they want to be with God's guidance
    d._____all of the above

3. Determining attainable goals can include:
    a._____decision-making
    b._____using a pros and cons list
    c._____talking it through with a fellow Christian
    d._____all of the above

4. Setting appropriate goals can include:
    a._____assessing how they match up with personal values
    b._____deciding which steps are necessary for your action plan and setting them
    c._____doing enough research to ensure goals align with Biblical principles
    d._____all of the above

5. Follow-up reflection of goals set can include:
    a._____reviewing logically
    b._____developing an action plan to meet the goal, regardless of Biblical principles
    c._____never reassessing the success of the process and effectiveness of the goal
    d._____all of the above

SKILL 3: Making Effective Decisions

DEFINITION: Going through a logical process of selecting the best solution from among the doable alternatives you are aware of. Making the best choice.

Now let's take the next step in critical thinking and examine the art of making decisions.

Following are steps in the process of decision-making:

- Decide what you are deciding
- Identify what the real problem is
- Choose how you want it to end
- Research your subject
- Evaluate information you have
- Consider options, what is realistic and doable for you
- Choose the practical outcome for you
- Develop the steps necessary to get there
- Move forward
- Decide to keep the result or start over

Following is a shortened version, using the acronym **REACH**, which you can use after you are comfortable with the process:

Research—ask-read-think

Evaluate—what is factual; not opinions

Analyze—without emotion; stick to the facts

Consider—possible outcomes; do a pros and cons list

Have at it—make your best decision; one you can live with tomorrow

ACTIVITY
1. **Beginning Level:** Consider the following scenario: Situation: You just received $30.00 for a birthday gift.   Decision: What is the most effective use for that money?
2. **Intermediate Level:**   In your group/partnership develop a thoughtful situation based on the setting and population.
3. **Advanced Level:**   In your group/partnership develop a thoughtful situation based on the setting and population.

Congratulations! By understanding and using these steps for decision-making and goal setting, you are moving forward in gathering life skills to propel you to where you want to be and doing what you want to do in your life.

BIBLICAL PRINCIPLE

*Discerning God's will for our lives and everyday decisions is
facilitated through an intimate relationship with Christ.*

Psalm 25:9 *He guides the humble in what is right and teaches them his way.*

Psalm 32:8 *I will instruct you and teach you in the way you should go; I will counsel you
and watch over you.*

Psalm 37:23 *If the LORD delights in a man's way, he makes his steps firm.*

Proverbs 2:1-6 *My Son, if you accept my words and store up my commands within you,
turning your ear to wisdom and applying your heart to understanding, and if you call out
for insight and cry aloud for understanding, and if you look for it as for silver and search
for it as for hidden treasure, then you will understand the fear of the LORD and find the
knowledge of God. For the LORD gives wisdom, and from his mouth come knowledge and
understanding.*

Proverbs 12:15 *The way of a fool seems right to him, but a wise man listens to advice.*

Isaiah 42:16 *I will lead the blind by ways they have not known, along unfamiliar paths I
will guide them; I will turn the darkness into light before them and make the rough places
smooth. These are the things I will do; I will not forsake them.*

Matthew 6:33 *But seek first his kingdom and his righteousness, and all these things will
be given to you as well.*

James 1:5 *If any of you lacks wisdom, he should ask God, who gives generously to all without
finding fault, and it will be given to him.*

MEMORY VERSE

Isaiah 30:21 *Whether you turn to the right or to the left, your ears will hear a voice behind
you, saying, "This is the way; walk in it."*

STUDY GUIDE

DEFINITION: Going through a logical process of selecting the best solution from among the doable alternatives you are aware of. Making the best choice.

Can you share a time in your life when you did not follow a logical process and the decision backfired?

This process requires following steps to ensure that you are making the most effective decision for your circumstances.

1. Think of one simple decision that you are trying to make. Do you have enough information to move forward to that place of the best decision? If not, where could you gather more information?

2. If you need more information, list three places (people) you could go to for that information:

1 _____

2 _____

3 _____

Now consider a more complicated pros and cons list for the decision you are considering.

Pros	Cons
1.	1.
2.	2.
3.	3.
4.	4.
5.	5.

OPTIONAL REVIEW FOR DECISION-MAKING

1. Decision-making is a process that:
   a. _____works best for folks who live by reacting with all-out emotions
   b. _____goes best when a coin is flipped for direction
   c. _____eliminates foolish guessing and has Biblical principles at the center
   d. _____none of the above

2. Effective decision-making:
   a._____helps move folks forward to the desired goal and regards Biblical principles
   b._____reflects having considered personal values
   c._____a & b
   d._____none of the above

3. The end goal of decision-making is:
   a._____having satisfied the most effective process in getting there
   b._____a choice that your friends really like
   c._____a choice that is emotion led
   d._____none of the above

4. Two things that could help to make a more effective decision are:
   a._____lots of money and lots of friends
   b._____using the REACH process, guided by the Word of God
   c._____doing what your research supports as right for you
   d._____b & c

5. Three significant components of an effective decision can include:
   a._____daily horoscope reading, Tarot cards, drawing from a hat
   b._____logic, research, and wisdom as gleaned from the Word of God
   c._____advice from rich friends, social acquaintances, your closest relative
   d._____all of the above

SKILL 4: Identifying Personal Values

DEFINITION: Those characteristics chosen to define who you are and what drives you.

I am:

Caring	Honest
Compassionate	Hopeful
Competent	Humble
Determined	Kind
Encouraging	Reality-based
Enthusiastic	Responsible
Giving	Wise
Happy	

BIBLICAL PRINCIPLE

God guides us how to live as His children, in this world with all peoples.

Gal 5:22-23 *But the fruit of the Spirit is love, joy, peace, longsuffering, kindness, goodness, faithfulness, gentleness, self-control.*

MEMORY VERSE

Gal 5:22-23 *But the fruit of the Spirit is love, joy, peace, longsuffering, kindness, goodness, faithfulness, gentleness, self-control.*

ACTIVITY
1. In your group/partnership, review your goals and values. Choose the top 5 values and then narrow to the primary value. At that point, identify what behavior reflects that in daily life. If appropriate, peers can support each other's belief with agreeing and why, from what they see lived out. Now draft a personal mission statement, using the goals and values to do so.
2. Write the final statement on an index card. Once completed keep it in a place where you will see it and remember that it is guiding every action, attitude, decision, feeling, and thought.

Congratulations! You are empowering yourself by taking charge of what you think, how you form your thoughts, thereby directing your progress to where you want to go, doing what you want to do, being who you want to be, all in God's will.

SKILL 5: Developing a Personal Value-based Mission Statement

BIBLICAL PRINCIPLE

God's word provides direction, purpose and instruction for the believer.

Psalm 37:3 (NKJV) *Trust in the LORD, and do good; Dwell in the land, and feed on His faithfulness.*

Proverbs 3:5-6 *Trust in the LORD with all your heart and lean not on your own understanding; in all your ways acknowledge him, and he will make your paths straight.*

Jeremiah 29:12-13 *Then you will call upon me and come and pray to me, and I will listen to you. You will seek me and find me when you seek me with all your heart.*

Matthew 25:21 *His master replied, "Well done, good and faithful servant! You have been faithful with a few things; I will put you in charge of many things. Come and share your master's happiness!"*

Romans 12:2 *Do not conform any longer to the pattern of this world, but be transformed by the renewing of your mind. Then you will be able to test and approve what God's will is – his good, pleasing and perfect will.*

Galatians 6:9 *Let us not become weary in doing good, for at the proper time we will reap a harvest if we do not give up.*

Philippians 2:3-4 *Do nothing out of selfish ambition or vain conceit, but in humility consider others better than yourselves. Each of you should look not only to your own interests, but also to the interests of others.*

Philippians 4:8 *Finally, brothers, whatever is true, whatever is noble, whatever is right, whatever is pure, whatever is lovely, whatever is admirable – if anything is excellent or praiseworthy – think about such things.*

2 Timothy 2:15 *Do your best to present yourself to God as one approved, a workman who does not need to be ashamed and who correctly handles the word of truth.*

MEMORY VERSE

Matthew 16:26-27 *What good will it be for a man if he gains the whole world, yet forfeits his soul? Or what can man give in exchange for his soul? For the Son of Man is going to come in his Father's glory with his angels, and then he will reward each person according to what he has done.*

WORK SHEET

DEFINITION: A statement that reflects your personal values, desired contributions and goals, guiding your life on every level.

Review your values, remembering which ones you have chosen, and which one defines you:

Personal Values:

- Caring
- Compassionate
- Competent
- Determined
- Encouraging
- Enthusiastic
- Giving
- Happy
- Honest
- Hopeful
- Humble
- Kind
- Reality-based
- Responsible
- Wise

Example: "To live my life to the fullest, with honesty, caring and love for God, myslef and others, while being reality-based, pursuing my personal and professional dreams with Jesus Christ at the center of all thoughts, feelings, attitudes, decisions, and actions."

Begin the first draft of your statement:

I will

_____

_____

_____

_____

_____

_____

Continue writing your statement here, and when it is how you want it, transfer to an index card to keep with you.

_____

_____

_____

_____

_____

_____

_____

_____

_____

_____

_____

_____

_____

_____

_____

_____

_____

_____

_____

_____

Appendices

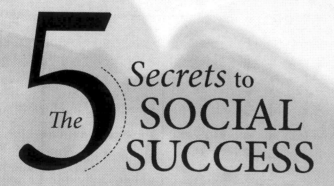

5
The Secrets to SOCIAL SUCCESS

with **Biblical Principles**   Dr. Lina W. Liken, C.A.P *with* **Cali Blalock, B.S.**

Assessment

Directions: After reading each pair of statements below, place a checkmark next to the one statement that most reflects your opinion. Once you have completed your assessment, your facilitator will lead a discussion about the points raised in the questions, and this process will serve as a lead-in to the training.

1. _____**a.** Making eye contact is only necessary when I am really interested in what someone is saying to me, and if there is nothing else going on around me that I am more interested in.

   _____**b.** Eye contact shows respect to the other person. It signals that I am present to what they are saying.

2. _____**a.** Listening to someone is easy and doesn't take paying attention. I can talk on the cell phone, read something, play a game, and just nod every now and then to show I am listening.

   _____**b.** Attending means I am focused on what you are saying, following along, and not being involved in any other activity at that time.

3. _____**a.** Being introduced to someone does not require any participation on my part. It doesn't matter if I look at them, shake their hand, or show any interest in the process.

   _____**b.** Using eye contact while being introduced makes the process more effective and me more social. It signals my participation with you and shows respect for you, the process and myself.

4. _____**a.** Being aware of or having good manners in my life has no real meaning and does not affect anything.

   _____**b.** Using good manners can help me be more socially successful. It shows that I do want to be part of the group I am in at that time, and know and honor the "rules of conduct."

5. _____**a.** Conversing means talking all the time, not regarding what anyone else has to say. When I have something to say, it is important and should be said first and if necessary, over other people who are talking.

_____**b.** Conversing is a social exchange of thoughts and comments. It is an opportunity for me to participate in a social process, learn more about other people and their ideas and demonstrate that I know how to be part of the process.

6. _____**a.** There is no respectful way to disagree with someone. When I am right, I am right.

_____**b.** I can disagree with someone and still be respectful to them. Being right all the time is not what it is about.

7. _____**a.** When there is conflict, someone must always win. I don't need to hear what anyone else has to say who does not agree with me.

_____**b.** Conflict may not always be resolved, yet there can be respect for each other while not agreeing.

8. _____**a.** If I want someone to agree with me, they must, or we can't have any conversation. Not agreeing with me shows that they don't like me. And if they don't want to do what I want to do, we can't be friends.

_____**b.** There may be times when I cannot persuade someone to agree with my point of view, yet we can respect each other.

9. _____**a.** Being aware of the feelings of someone else does not matter to me. How they feel is their problem and I don't care.

_____**b.** It can be helpful to recognize the feelings of another person. Sometimes what they are feeling is not how they look, and I may react incorrectly based on my assumption.

10._____**a.** Getting upset in a conversation shows others how I feel and makes me right. Being loud helps me to be the stronger person in the conversation.

_____**b.** Being able to keep calm in all situations shows respect for myself and strengthens my social skills.

11._____**a.** There are times when I am talking to someone that they may not want me to have physical contact with them. Putting my arm around their shoulder can be uncomfortable for them.

_____**b.** There are more respectful ways to reach out to someone during a casual conversation.

12. ____**a.** Making people laugh is always fun and it doesn't matter how I do it. Telling jokes and making funny comments helps me to be the center of the action and I like how it feels, even if someone else is offended by what I say or how I say it.

____**b.** There are topics in funny stories and jokes that can make others uncomfortable and really aren't funny. Taking into consideration the feelings of others will ensure that my social skills protect me from upsetting or insulting someone.

13. ____**a.** When I set goals it always takes the fun out of what I want to do.

____**b.** Having goals helps me get to where I want to be. When I have a goal, I can move forward with purpose.

14. ____**a.** Tossing a coin can be an effective way to decide what to do. It is a waste of time to do research about my choices. Whatever happens I will be able to work it out. When I have a feeling, like something or really want it, that makes my decision easy.

____**b.** Using a disciplined process for making decisions can lead to more successful outcomes. When there are no or few negative consequences to my decisions, I can be more effective in my life.

15. ____**a.** The words I use when I speak can influence my attitudes. Painting the word pictures sends messages to my brain about how I really feel toward something or someone.

____**b.** Negative words never impact on my mind.

16. ____**a.** Values are what I decide are important to who I am and how I live.

____**b.** It is better to change my values in every situation. Sometimes I could lose out on an opportunity if I stuck to what I valued.

17. ____**a.** When I know who I am, what I stand for, and why, I can be more successful in life. Being successful means living true to who I am.

____**b.** It is better to not bother with deciding who I want to be, just live each day with no guidelines or goals, enjoying the "life of drifting along." Being socially successful includes being responsible to my values, and if I do that all the time, I might miss out on something.

Answers for Chapter Reviews

I. COMMUNICATION

SKILL 1: Establishing Appropriate Eye Contact

REVIEW & ANSWER KEY

*Believers should purpose to convey confidence, security,
honor, and respect to those with whom they interact.*

Fill in the Blanks:
1. Matthew 6:21-23 describes the eye as the **LAMP** of the **BODY**.

2. According to Romans 12:10, how should we treat others?
    a. with great trepidation
    b. with disrespect
    c. with hostility
    d. **with honor and devotion**

3. According to 1Peter 2:17, whom should we respect?
    a. our immediate family
    b. those in authority
    c. God
    d. **all of the above**

4. *Write:*
1Peter 2:17 from memory on the lines below.
"Show proper respect to everyone, love the family of believers, fear God, honor the emperor."

I. COMMUNICATION

SKILL 2: Understanding Hearing, Listening, and Attending

<u>**REVIEW & ANSWER KEY**</u>

Wisdom is an essential component of Christian character. Attaining wisdom is accomplished through learning the skills of hearing, listening, and attending.

1. *Fill in the Blanks:*
According to Proverbs 4:1, what do we gain as a result of paying attention?

    a. headache   **b. understanding**   c. friendships   d. money

2. *List:*
The three pieces of advice, found in James 1:19, which could be implemented when we are engaged in conversations with others.

    1. **Be quick to listen.**
    2. **Be slow to speak.**
    3. **Be slow to anger.**

3. *Write:*
Matthew 13:23 from memory on the lines below.

    "But the seed falling on good soil refers to someone who hears the word and understands it. This is the one who produces a crop, yielding a hundred, sixty or thirty times what was sown."

I. COMMUNICATION

SKILL 3: Conversing

REVIEW & ANSWER KEY

Christ engaged his audience with speech filled with purpose, authority, wisdom, and compassion. His words instructed, corrected, enlightened, edified, and encouraged his listeners.

1. *Fill in the Blank:*
According to Psalm 19:14, the words we speak should first be pleasing to ***the Lord***.

2. *True or **False***
Ephesians 4:29 teaches that our words should be used to express our opinions and for praising ourselves.

3.   *Circle the Correct Letter:*
What is the promise of Psalm 34:12-13 if we keep our tongues from evil and our lips from speaking lies?

      a.   we would enjoy many good days
      a.   our financial status will improve
      b.   many will come to seek our counsel
      c.   all of the above

4. *Fill in the Blanks:*
According to James 3:9-10, ***praise*** and ***cursing*** should not come out of the same mouth.

5. *Circle the Correct Letter:*
Proverbs 15:7 explains that a wise person disperses _____ with their words.
    a. sarcasm   b. insult   c. attitude   **d. knowledge**

II. CIVILITY

SKILL 1: Using Appropriate Humor in Conversation

REVIEW & ANSWER KEY

Humor is a gift from God designed to uplift and build camaraderie.

1. *Write:*
Proverbs 17:22 from memory on the lines below:
   "A cheerful heart is good medicine, but a crushed spirit dries up the bones."

2. *Circle the Correct Letter:*
How does Proverbs 26:18-19 describe someone who is deceitful and says, "I was only joking!"?

   a. A comedian   b. A good friend   c. A Christian   **d. A madman**

3. *Fill in the Blanks:*
"Pleasant words are like a honeycomb, **sweetness** to the **soul** and **health** to the **bones**."

4. *Circle the Correct Letter:*
According to Matthew 15:10, what makes a person unclean?

   a. what comes out of his mouth
   b. going without a shower
   c. what goes into his mouth
   d. the food he eats

II. CIVILITY

SKILL 2: Disagreeing Respectfully

REVIEW & ANSWER KEY

Believers have the assurance of the infallible Word of God. God's Word
is eternal and authoritative. In the midst of a disagreement, we must rest
in the knowledge that God will make His way known and final.

1. *Circle the Correct Letter:*
According to Proverbs 15:1, how should you respond when another individual is expressing their anger toward you?
   a. You should respond with anger
   b. You should attempt to defend yourself
   c. **You should respond with a gentle answer**
   d. None of the above

2. *Fill in the Blanks:*
Philippians 3:15 teaches that **God** will make all things clear to those who are **mature** in the event of a disagreement.

3. *Write:*
Titus 3:9 from memory on the lines below:
   "But avoid foolish controversies and genealogies and arguments and quarrels about the law, because these are unprofitable and useless."

II. CIVILITY

SKILL 3: Resolving Conflict

<u>**REVIEW & ANSWER KEY**</u>

We are identified as believers by our willingness and ability
to promote and seek peace and reconciliation.

1. *List:*
The behaviors stated in Ephesians 4:31-32 that we, as believers, should eliminate from our interactions with others.
   Bitterness, Rage, Anger, Brawling, Slander, Malice

2. *Circle the Correct Letter:*
According to Proverbs 13:10, what sin is the source of all strife/conflict?
         a. gluttony   **b. pride**   c. lying   d. anger

How does Proverbs 29:11 describe someone who keeps himself under control?
         a. wise   b. foolish   c. ignorant   d. weak

3. *Write:*
Matthew 5:9 from memory on the lines below:
   "Blessed are the peacemakers, for they will be called sons of God."

4. ***True*** *or False*

5. *Write:*
Luke 6:28-29 instructs us to bless those who curse us and pray for those who mistreat us.

II. CIVILITY

SKILL 4: Remaining Calm

REVIEW & ANSWER KEY

Believers must demonstrate soberness in their approach to life by not allowing their emotions to master them or dictate their behavior.

1. *List:*
The fruit of the Spirit found in Galatians 5:22-23:
   Love, Joy, Peace, Patience, Kindness, Goodness, Faithfulness, Gentleness, Self-Control

2. *Circle the Correct Letter:*
Proverbs 29:11 describes someone who does not keep his emotions under control as a:

   a. genius   **b. fool**   c. lawyer   d. hero

3. ***True*** *or False*
Being self-controlled and alert protects us against our enemy, the devil, who prowls around looking for someone to devour.

4. *Fill in the Blanks:*
   *"For God did not give us a spirit of **timidity** but a spirit of **power** of **love** and of **self-discipline**." 2 Timothy 1:7*

III. HUMILITY

SKILL 1: Introducing Self and Others

REVIEW & ANSWER KEY

*Setting a tone of peace and wellness enables the believer to
establish a godly witness and trust within a relationship,
thus providing an opportunity for sharing his/her faith.*

1. *Circle the Correct Letter* after you *Read* 1 Samuel 25:5-6: What three blessings did David wish for Nabal in his greeting?
   a. **Long life, health to him and his household, and health to everything that belongs to him.**
   b. Financial security, good relationships, and love.
   c. Wisdom, love, and faith.
   d. Winning the Lotto, fame and fortune, and happiness.

According to Matthew 10:11-13, what should you do upon entering a home and what should rest upon the home during your stay?
   a. Turn on the TV (your feet)
   b. **Greet the hosts (your peace)**
   c. Demand a meal (chaos)
   d. Make a phone call (turmoil)

2. *List:*
Three positive characteristics of a greeting:
   Answers will vary but should reflect what was discussed.

III. HUMILITY

SKILL 2: Living With Good Manners

REVIEW & ANSWER KEY

*The sacred duty of the believer is to treat others
with respect, love, kindness, and hospitality.*

1. *List:*
According to Colossians 3:12, the characteristics we should posses as believers are:
   Compassion, Kindness, Humility, Gentleness, Patience

2. *Write:*
Matthew 7:12 from memory on the lines below.
   "So in everything, do to others what you would have them do to you, for this sums up the law and the prophets."

3. *Match:*
The acrostic letters for MANNERS with the correct verses:

M	1. Meet-18:2 Meal-18:8
A	2. Accept/Acknowledge-18:3
N	3. Noble -18:5
N	4. Notable-18:18
E	5. Extra Mile-18:5
R	6. Respect-18:4
S	7. Servant heart-18:2

4. *Fill in the Blank:*
Hebrews 13:2 states that by entertaining strangers we might unknowingly entertain **ANGELS.**

III. HUMILITY

SKILL 3: Showing Respect

REVIEW & ANSWER KEY

Christians must be 'others focused' and humble.

1. *Fill in the Blanks:*
Read Leviticus 19:32 and Ephesians 6:2-3. What two groups of people are we commanded to show honor and respect to?
> **The Elderly** and **Parents**

2. *Circle the Correct Letter*:
According to Leviticus 19:32, what is one example of demonstrating respect to the elderly.
   a. Turning your back to them
   b. Waving hello from your seat
   c. Applauding their presence
   d. Standing up in their presence

3. *Write:*
Philippians 2:3 from memory on the lines below.
> ***"Do nothing out of selfish ambition or vain conceit, but in humility consider others better than yourselves."***

4. ***True*** *or False:*
According to Ephesians 6:3, honoring your father and mother will promise to result in a long and prosperous life.

IV. RELATIONSHIPS

SKILL 1: Reading Emotions

REVIEW & ANSWER KEY

Believers must exercise discernment to determine the emotional needs
of an individual and minister accordingly.

1. *Circle the Correct Letter:*
According to 2 Corinthians 1:3-4, how can you use the comfort you receive from God during your own troubles?
       a. You can journal your feelingsb
       b. You can ignore the needs of others
       c. You can pray for them
       d. **You can comfort those in trouble**

2. *Fill in the Blank:*
Hebrews 3:13 instructs us to **encourage** one another daily.

3. *Write:*
According to Proverbs 12:25, how can you cheer someone up who is anxious?
   You can cheer someone who is anxious up by sharing a kind word with them.

4. *True or **False:***
Romans 12:1 tells us to rejoice with those who mourn and mourn with those who rejoice.

IV. RELATIONSHIPS

SKILL 2: Persuading Others

REVIEW & ANSWER KEY

Believers must be prepared to persuade people to respond positively to the Scripture's message of grace and calling to commit their life to Christ.

1. *Circle the Correct Letter:*
Matthew 28:19 commands us to:
  - a. **Make disciples, baptize others, teach obedience**
  - b. Make friends, socialize often, relax
  - c. Read the Bible, pray for others, be helpful
  - d. All of the above

2. *Fill in the Blanks:*
According to Proverbs 18:21, our words have the power to bring **death** or **life** to others.

1 Peter 3:15-16 instructs us to be **open-minded** and **agreeable** when explaining to others the reason for the hope we have in Christ.

3. ***True*** *or False:*
According to Matthew 7:28, the crowds were amazed at Jesus' teachings because he spoke as one who had authority.

IV. RELATIONSHIPS

SKILL 3: Demonstrating Appropriate Affection during Conversations

REVIEW & ANSWER KEY

Believers would be wise to apply healthy boundaries during personal interactions with others in order to guard against temptations and misunderstandings.

1. *Circle the Correct Letter:*
According to 1Thessalonians 4:3-7, how can we avoid wronging or taking advantage of others while interacting in a social relationship or setting?
   a. **Behaving in a manner that is holy and honorable**
   b. Avoiding others
   c. Behaving in a manner that is rude and obnoxious
   d. b and c

2. *Write:*
What is the promise for the pure in heart, stated in Matthew 5:8?
   The pure in heart will see God.

3. *List*:
5 characteristics of **love** found in 1 Corinthians 13:4-7:
   Any 5 of the Following Responses Will Be Correct:
   - *patience*
   - *kindness*
   - *not envious*
   - *not boastful*
   - *not proud*
   - *not rude*
   - *not self-seeking*
   - *not easily angered*
   - *keeps no records of wrongs*
   - *does not delight in evil*
   - *rejoices with the truth*
   - *protective*
   - *always trusts*
   - *always perseveres*

V. WISDOM

SKILL 1: Adopting and Demonstrating a Positive Attitude

REVIEW & ANSWER KEY

As Christ encouraged, enlightened and edified his listeners, His positive attitude shone through his every thought, feeling and action.

Fill in the Blanks:

1. According to Proverbs 15:13, *A happy heart makes the* **face** *cheerful, but heartache crushes the* **spirit** *.*

One way to influence attitude is **thinking** and **speaking** in positive phrases.

Let us hold unswervingly to the hope we profess, for he who promised is _____ **faithful** *.*

What is the promise made in **Hebrews 10:23**
God is faithful.

2. ***True*** *or False:*
_____. According to Matthew 7:28, the crowds were amazed at Jesus' teachings because he spoke as one who had authority.

Optional Review Answers

Quiz for Decision-Making

1. Decision-making is a process that:
   c. eliminates foolish guessing and has Biblical principles at the center

2. Effective decision-making:
   a. helps move life forward to the desired goal, with regard to Biblical principles

3. The end goal of decision-making is:
   a. having satisfied the most effective process in getting there

4. Two things that could help to make a more effective decision are:
   b. using the REACH process, guided by the Word of God

5. Three significant components of an effective decision can include:
   b. logic, research, wisdom as gleaned from the Word of God

Quiz for Goal Setting

1. Goals can be defined as:
   b. the results of sound and effective decision-making

2. Having goals is appropriate for:
   d. all of the above

3. Determing attainable goals can incude:
   d. all of the above

4. Setting appropriate goals can include:
   d. all of the above

5. Follow-up reflection of goals set can include:
   a. reviewing logically

Notes